# Living with Plants

# Living with Plants

## A BOOK OF HOME DECORATING & PLANT CARE

by WILLIAM S. HAWKEY

Illustrated by Tim Shortt
Photography by Norman McGrath and Douglas Mesney

WILLIAM MORROW & COMPANY, INC.     New York

Printed in the United States of America.


1   2   3   4   5   78   77   76   75   74


Designed by Leslie Adalman/Craven & Evans, Creative Graphics


Library of Congress Cataloging in Publication Data

Hawkey, William S
 Living with plants.

 Bibliography: p.
 1.   House plants in interior decoration.   I.   Title.


SB419.H34        747'.9        74-7079


ISBN 0-688-00277-3

To my children, Beth, Bill,
Adam, Robin, and Renn,
without whom this book would have
been done a long time ago.

# Acknowledgments

I want to thank illustrator Tim Shortt who drew the pictures
and gave the book its look; photographer Doug Mesney who put
in long greenhouse hours getting dracaenas to say "cheese," and
photographer Norman McGrath whose interior work is already
well known; they both lend a special elegance to this book; my
agent Knox Burger who got things off the ground, and my editor
Narcisse Chamberlain whose know-how, patience, and fine ideas
made this book a reality.

Also thanks to horticulturalists Emanuel Shemin, Ina Bass,
Charles Henry, and Pat Toscano who supplied answers, advice,
and plants; to building super Frank Soto who set me up in a
damp, cold basement room . . . the perfect New York writer's
garret; to plant grower Larry Vogt who put up with long
photographic sessions and endless questions; and to indoor-plant
specialists Dick Waite and Roger Wohrle who supplied
photographic locations and expert advice and their own magic
greenhouse.

# Contents

# List of Color Pictures

# Living with Plants

# Part One

# The Interior Environment

and live plants were little seen indoors. But formal arrangements of silken or dried flowers as well as fresh bouquets from the cutting gardens graced the carved mantels and lowboys.

During the early part of the eighteenth century upward of five thousand species of tropical plants were introduced into Europe, and in the nineteenth century the great botanical era reached its height with plants arriving from the Americas, India, Africa, and Australia.

In early America, our forefathers had little time in their struggle for survival for cultivation of any plants that could not be eaten. But it would be hard to imagine a housewife who didn't manage to cultivate some flowers in her kitchen garden, along with herbs and lanky geraniums in her kitchen window. When homes became larger, during the Colonial and Federal periods, and homeowners became wealthier, semitropical plants probably found their way north from the Southern plantations. Finally, during the Victorian period, the great influx of imported, exotic plants began in earnest. There was hardly a Victorian room worthy of the name that did not have several gracefully arching palms lounging against the dark-stained paneling. And for the cooler rooms and porches there were feathery, lime-green ferns trailing their lacy fronds over elaborately carved pedestals.

Today you can draw on any of these historic styles when you develop your decorating schemes, but you don't have to be bound by the historical use of plants. Analyze your furniture and interior space with an architect's eye. Establish a philosophical point of view about the size and balance of, for instance, your Japanese or Shaker chest and then select a companion plant that best expresses or complements that point of view. Large plants, growing in containers, are not often seen in classic Japanese interiors. Usually an exquisite bonsai or an ingeniously conceived and executed arrangement of dried or living flowers and foliage will be the sole connection

to the outside world of nature. But if you are decorating in the Japanese style, and you don't insist on being a purist, why not take advantage of the very oriental-looking *Dracaena marginata* or the ming-tree? The Shaker influence, too, if followed to the letter, would preclude the use of houseplants. But even the balanced, functional Shaker look would be complemented by the presence of a tall member of the cactus family. Tall, tropical-looking plants and smaller ferns work well against the dark woods of Spanish-style furniture. Scandinavian interiors generally have a "designed" look, and plants of the same shape and size placed in well-designed groupings can be effective architectural elements in themselves. Contemporary houses, with their expanses of glass, are ideally suited to growing plants in interior environments. In these houses, where the emphasis is on functional space, plants not only look handsome but can work as space definers.

The following chapters will explore the interior of the house, room by room, to show how plants, with their many different personalities, can create exciting new effects for today's interior decoration.

### Plants as Living Architecture

Plants, like humans, come in all shapes and sizes and colors. There isn't an odd-shaped nook or cranny in your home that couldn't take a plant of some sort. Let's suppose that you've got a strange corner over there next to the fireplace that's too crowded for a sofa, but looks bare without something. A six-hundred-dollar Chippendale tilt-top table might do the trick, but so might a forty-dollar specimen *Ficus nitida*.

The plants listed in the next chapter are grouped into three sizes: tall, medium, and small. So now, when you stand back and squint at that empty corner, and you say to yourself, "Hmmmmm, I need something about as tall as I am in that spot," you can turn to the plants listed under "Tall" to find all of the recommended possibilities ranging in size from three feet on up. These plants, such as schefflera, and some of the dracaenas and palms, will be likely candidates for free-standing accents, area definers, and that barren corner.

Plants listed under "Medium" are from one foot to three feet in height. Plants in this size range are suitable for tabletops, as container plants, as free-standing accents, for use in groups with either plants of the same size or in combination with tall plants. Rex begonias, cacti, pittosporum, and dieffenbachia are just a few of the plants in the medium-size category. Others will include less mature specimens of plants which we usually consider as tall.

"Small" plants are under a foot in height. They may be used in terrariums, containers, planters, miniature landscapes, and in hanging baskets. Many of them will work well in planters with medium-sized plants.

All of the plants discussed in this book have been selected for their tolerance for average household conditions. All of the plants are described in terms of their individual needs, as well as in terms of their personalities. The rest is up to you.

schefflera

anthurium

*Dicksonia squarrosa*

aeonium

# 2. Plants at a Glance

## How to Use This Book

There are plenty of good books about houseplants, but most of them are "plant-oriented" and are written and organized for the enthusiastic home gardener. *Living with Plants* goes beyond plant care and the use of plants as accessories, and shows you how to create a new kind of interior harmony by selecting plants for their architectural, esthetic, and personal qualities; and how to live comfortably with plants as companions.

One of the problems an author runs into when writing a book about plants is whether or not to use those tongue-twisting Latin names. They have an advantage in being universal and specific, but reading them in a book like this can be a real chore. Common names are easily read and remembered and have personality. Unfortunately, though, several different plants often will have the same common name, and many common names change from region to region. So I've used both in this book, leaning a bit toward the common names in the beginning chapters, and lapsing into occasional Latin as your familiarity with these names progresses along with the book. Plants in Chapter 2, Plants at a Glance, are listed alphabetically, and according to size category, by their Latin names. Common names are also given for each plant. In the Appendix is a common-name/Latin-name glossary if you get stuck. Good luck.

There is a lot of how-to information in Chapter 3, The Living Room, that pertains to the other rooms in the house as well. So read Chapter 3 from beginning to end even if the living room isn't your number-one project. And if you find an idea you like in a room chapter other than the one you're interested in working with at the moment, go ahead and tailor it to your needs.

Each plant picture and plant description in this chapter is accompanied by a set of symbols indicating temperature, light, and moisture requirements. They are all explained in Chapter 13, Plant Care; you should familiarize yourself with them so that you can tell at a glance whether or not a plant would be happy in the location you have picked out for it:

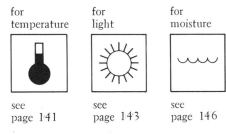

for temperature — see page 141

for light — see page 143

for moisture — see page 146

Finally, if some of the terms or information in Part Two (the room chapters) gets too technical for you, look the subject up in the Index. It will refer you to the appropriate pages in Part Three, where horticultural material is fully explained.

# TALL PLANTS

**Araucaria Excelsa**
**Norfolk Island pine.** Looks like a Christmas tree.
Deep-green needles, lighter toward tips of branches.
Formal, elegant, stately. Use with dark, polished
wood, sculpture, leather furniture.

**Beaucarnea Recurvata**
**Pony-tail palm, elephant's-foot tree.** Plumes of
¾-inch-wide leaves atop slender trunk which swells
into interesting bulbous shape at soil level. Good
specimen plant. Use with Victoriana.

**Brassaia Actinophylla**
**Schefflera.** Small plants bear 3 to 5 leaflets per stem.
As plant grows, stems develop up to 16 leaflets, each
a foot long. Massive yet delicate. Use with wicker,
contemporary furniture, or antiques.

**Cereus Peruvianus**
**Tree-cactus.** Powdery, bluish-green columns with 6 to
9 ribs. Freely branching from base. Few brown spines.
Whitish flowers. Available in small–medium sizes.

**Caryota Mitis**
**Fishtail-palm.** Many stems arching into 4-foot-long
fronds which send out fishtail-shaped leaflets.

**Chamaedorea Elegans**
**Neanthe bella palm.** A tree-palm in miniature.
Slow-growing. Thin stems bear rosettes of small,
featherlike leaves of deep green.

**Chamaedorea Erumpens**
**Bamboo-palm.** Bushy, erect clusters of bamboolike
stems. Short, drooping fronds with papery,
deep-green, recurved leaflets. Informal, airy.

**Chamaerops Humilis**
**European fan-palm.** Stiff, fan-shaped leaves sprouting
from short, rough, fibrous trunk. Gray-green. Usually
available under 5 feet tall.

**Chrysalidocarpus Lutescens**
**Areca-palm, butterfly-palm.** Long, graceful, yellowish
stems. Glossy, yellow-green foliage. Feathery.
Somewhat fragile near kids.

**Cyathea Arborea**
**Tree-fern.** Feathery, fernlike, lemon-green fronds.
Ideal for a tropical look. Use in background, with
smaller plants in front.

**Cycas Revoluta**
**Sago-palm.** Stout trunk a few inches tall. Iron-hard,
leathery, deep-green fronds grow upward, curving at
tips. Good floor model. Can withstand abuse.

**Dizygotheca Elegantissima**
**False-aralia.** Upright, reaching 5 or more feet.
Fingerlike leaves slender and coppery, changing to
very dark green in maturity. Lacy form.

**Dracaena Marginata**
Slender, gracefully curving, grayish-tan trunks topped
with dense rosettes of deep-green, leathery leaves
with red edges. Oriental-looking.

**Dracaena Massangeana**
Leaves look like the leaves of corn. They form in
rosettes of laxly curving clusters atop long, slender,
straight stems. Long canes useful in narrow spaces.
Large specimens palmlike.

**Ficus Benjamina**
**Weeping-fig.** Beautiful and graceful. Leathery, glossy,
deep-green leaves. Drooping habit. Good with
sculpture, art, contemporary furniture.

**Ficus Elastica Decora**
**Rubber-tree.** A bold plant. Broad, large leaves.
Deep-green, midrib red underneath. Sheath of
growing tip is red. Massive form. Needs room, or it
can overpower other elements.

**Ficus Lyrata (F. Pandurata)**
**Fiddle-leaf fig.** Large, thick, leathery leaves shaped
like highly polished violins, quilted and wavy, with
yellow-green veins. Good with rich, dark woods.

**Ficus Nitida**
**Indian laurel.** A thick-topped tree with neat,
"clipped," outdoor appearance. Leaves are glossy, rich
green, oval, and 3 inches long. Contemporary and
straightforward looking.

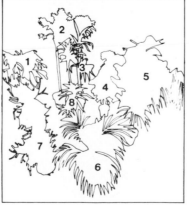

## Tall Plants

1. *Chamaedorea erumpens* palm
2. *Ficus nitida*
3. *Cordyline terminalis* tricolor
4. Podocarpus
5. Adonidia palm
6. Kentia-palm
7. Pencil-cactus
8. *Dracaena Warneckii*

## Tall Plants

1. *Ficus exotica benjamina*
2. *Dracaena Massangeana*
3. *Dracaena marginata*
4. Rhapis palm

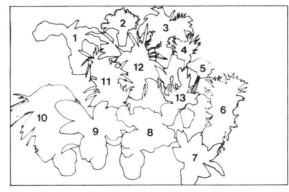

## Medium Plants

1. **Dieffenbachia**
2. *Crassula argentea*
3. *Phoenix Roebelenii* palm
4. **Yucca**
5. *Aralia chinensis*
6. **Pleomele**
7. **Schismatoglottis**
8. *Ficus pandurata*
9. **Spathiphyllum**
10. *Aralia elegantissima*
11. *Dracaena Warneckii*
12. *Dracaena 'Janet Craig'*
13. *Euphorbia lactea*

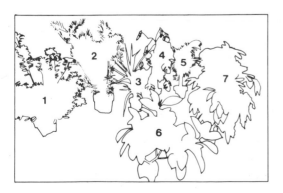

## Medium Plants

1. **Pittosporum**
2. **Podocarpus**
3. **Yucca**
4. *Monstera deliciosa*
5. **Areca-palm**
6. *Ficus decora*
7. **Schefflera**

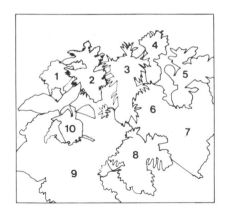

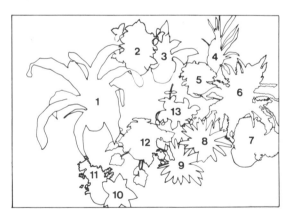

## Medium Plants

1. Ivy
2. *Araucaria excelsa*
3. Pleomele
4. Croton
5. *Clusia rosea*
6. Ivy
7. Ivy
8. *Philodendron Selloum*
9. Ivy
10. Dieffenbachia

## Small Plants

1. Bromeliad
2. Coleus
3. Philodendron
4. Sansevieria
5. Begonia
6. *Nephrolepis Whitmanii*
7. Pittosporum
8. Bromeliad
9. Bromeliad
10. Aphelandra
11. Crassula
12. *Tolmeia Menziesii*
13. *Hoya carnosa*

Small Plants

1. **Bromeliads**
2. **Nephrolepis** fern
3. *Asplenium Nidus* fern

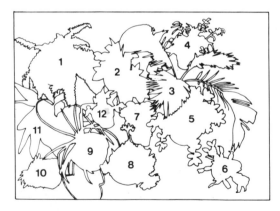

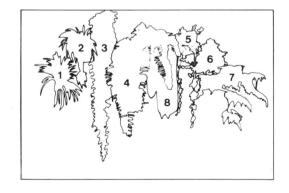

## Small Plants

1. **Nephrolepis exaltata Bostoniensis**
2. **Fatsia japonica**
3. **Kentia-palm**
4. **Pteris fern**
5. Pilea
6. **Schlumbergera Bridgesii**
7. Peperomia
8. Begonia
9. Beaucarnea
10. Pteris
11. Aglaonema
12. **Syngonium Wendlandii**

## Hanging Plants

1. Bromeliad
2. Chlorophytum
3. Episcia
4. **Polypodium subauriculatum**
5. Episcia
6. Peperomia
7. Davallia fern
8. Rhipsalis

## A Grouping of Plants

1. **Orchid**
2. **Nephrolepis fern**
3. **Orchids**
4. **Orchid**
5. **Orchid**
6. **Dieffenbachia**
7. **Bromeliad**
8. **Maranta**

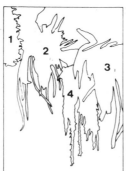

## Hanging Plants

1. **Tradescantia**
2. **Bromeliad**
3. **Orchid**
4. **Davallia fern**

**Howea Forsteriana**
**Kentia-palm, paradise-palm.** Long, graceful fronds arching up and out. New leaves at the top grow larger than those below. Hardy, slow-growing. Formal and Victorian.

**Philodendron Panduriforme**
**Fiddle-leaf philodendron.** Dull, olive-green, fiddle-shaped leaves. Usually sold climbing on bark.

**Philodendron Pertusum**
**Split-leaf philodendron.** Actually juvenile stage of *Monstera deliciosa*. Deeply notched, almost round leaves 8 to 12 inches long. Light green upon opening, maturing to deep green. Usually vines on bark slab.

**Philodendron Selloum**
**Saddle-leaf philodendron.** Self-heading form. Leaves are a foot and a half long by a foot wide, and it spreads out. Good for large rooms. Massive shape, but finely cut interior details.

**Pittosporum Tobira**
**Japanese pittosporum, mock-orange.** Bush form, somewhat flat-topped. Thick, lustrous, green leaves grow in whorls. Sometimes in the spring, if you're lucky, look for tiny white flowers which smell like orange blossoms.

**Pleomele Reflexa**
**Pleomele.** The short leathery leaves cluster densely around the willowy stem. Needs support, or the stem will bend at the top. A variegated variety, 'Song of India', has leaves which are margined with bands of yellow or cream.

**Podocarpus Macrophylla Maki**
**Southern yew, Chinese podocarpus.** Waxy, blackish-green, 1½ to 3 inches long, needlelike leaves. Looks like an evergreen and can be pruned like one.

**Polyscias Balfouriana**
**Ming-tree, aralia.** Shiny, dark-green leaflets, shaped like the leaves of the violet. Some varieties have milky-green leaves edged in deep green, and others have white borders and dark-green centers. *P. fruticosa* has lacy, finely cut foliage and is very Oriental and elegant.

### Rhapis Excelsa
**Large-lady-palm.** Fan-shaped leaves, 1 foot wide, are borne on slender, bamboolike stems which join together and are matted with coarse fiber. A durable potted palm.

### Veitchia (Adonidia) Merrillii
**Christmas palm, Manila palm.** Bright-green fronds arch gracefully from the top of the slender, ringed trunk. Useful as a specimen, or in concert with smaller plants.

### Yucca
**Spanish bayonet.** Stiff rosette of thick, sharp pointed leaves. Don't bump into them!

## MEDIUM-SIZED PLANTS

### Aglaonema Commutatum
**Chinese evergreen.** Will grow in dark corners and also in plain water. Some have dark-green, lance-shaped leaves, others have leaves marked with white or silver. Very tough plant.

### Aloe Vera
**Medicine-plant.** Pulp used to heal burns and sores. Rosettes of succulent leaves sometimes reaching 2 feet long. Gray-green and powdery-looking.

### Aspidistra Elatior
**Cast-iron plant.** Can stand almost anything but with care will grow into handsome plant. Arching leaves have white and green stripes in the variegated variety.

### Aucuba Japonica Variegata
**Gold-dust tree.** Large, shiny, green leaves dusted with golden yellow. Other varieties sport different combinations of green and yellow.

### Caladium
**Fancy-leaved caladium.** Striking, colorful foliage. Big, heart-shaped leaves up to 2 feet long. Red, pink, silver, white, green.

### Cibotium Schiedei
**Mexican tree-fern.** Fernlike fronds spread 2 to 3 feet outward. Good for pedestals. Will grow in plain water, with rocks for support.

### Citrus Mitis
**Calamondin orange.** Fruit looks like a 1½-inch orange. Use in marmalade. Good dining-table plant.

### Clusia Rosea
Thick, leathery, deep-green leaves shaped like paddles.

### Cordyline Terminalis Bicolor
**Hawaiian ti.** Leaves a deep, metallic green edged in pink. Loves high humidity and will grow in plain water.

### Crassula Argentea
**Chinese jade.** Takes the form of plump, fat-trunked trees. Leaves thick, glossy, jade-green, sometimes edged in red. Good for miniature landscapes.

### Croton
Fantastic leaf shapes and colorings ranging through yellows, coppers, greens, rusts, reds, oranges, browns, and ivory. The colors can appear as blotches or veinings, or can color the whole leaf.

### Dieffenbachia
**Dumb-cane.** Thick stems are topped with large, oblong leaves. Some are deep green with cream-white bands and blotches. Others have greenish-yellow leaves with green-and-white spots. *Caution:* the leaves and stems are poisonous.

### Dracaena Sanderiana
**Sander's dracaena.** Very hardy, will grow in plain water. Leaves 8 to 10 inches long, gray-green with white edges.

### Euonymus Japonicus
**Evergreen euonymus.** Inch-long, bright-green leaves. The 'Silver Queen' variety has green leaves edged in white. Others have yellow edges.

### Euphorbia
Some look like cacti. The milk-striped euphorbia looks like a green candelabrum. Crown-of-thorns has red blooms at the tips of the branches.

### Fatshedera
**Tree-ivy.** An accidental cross between an Irish ivy and a Japanese ivy produced this shrub. Will grow to 3 feet, with support. Leaves deep green, to 10 inches across. Looks like ivy.

### Fatsia Japonica
**Maple-leaf.** Shiny green leaves up to 16 inches across. Grows to 4 feet but can be pruned back.

### Ligustrum Japonicum Texanum
**Wax-leaf privet, Texas privet.** Compact. Thick, glossy, dark-green leaves. Can be shaped. Very tough.

### Pandanus
**Screw-pine.** Thin, curving leaves in rosettes, 3 inches wide narrowing to point. Light- to deep-green lined with cream. A stem develops as the plant matures and sends out supporting roots beneath the rosette. *Caution: the leaves are sharp.*

### Philodendron Wendlandii
**Wendland's philodendron.** Thick, waxy-green leaves, 12 to 18 inches long, rising in a rosette like the bird's-nest fern. May blossom indoors.

### Phoenix Roebelenii
**Miniature date-palm, pigmy date-palm.** Graceful, arching, 1–2-foot leaves with 7–9-inch green leaflets. Feathery. Comes in small size, too, which is good for terrariums.

### Platycerium Bifurcatum
**Staghorn-fern.** An "air plant," it usually comes attached to moisture-retaining basket or bark for wall hanging. Unusual and majestic.

### Sansevieria
**Snake-plant.** Erect with leathery, lancelike, concave leaves up to 4 feet long. Grass-green to dark-green banded with light-green to gray-green. An old favorite. Very tough.

### Spathiphyllum
Thin, leathery, lancelike, glossy-green leaves. White, papery flowers, shaped like anthuriums, on reedlike stems. Tolerates low light.

## SMALL PLANTS

### Acorus
**Sweet-flag.** Grasslike. Use in terrariums.

### Adiantum Tenerum Wrightii
**Fan-maidenhair fern.** A cloud of green coins on black, wirelike stems. Dainty.

**Agave**
Century-plant. Dense, many-leaved rosette.
Slow-growing.

**Aphelandra**
Zebra-plant. Favorite florist's item. Clusters of yellow
flowers on a spike. Leaves dimpled and glossy green,
veined in white. After the flower goes, the foliage
is most useful.

**Asplenium Nidus-Avis**
Bird's-nest fern. Lime-green fronds growing upward
in a rosette. Tolerant of dry air.

**Begonia**
Many kinds. Rex begonias have large leaves in colors
ranging from pinks, reds, silvers, and rusts to
purple-black. Fibrous-rooted begonias flower freely.
Hanging-basket begonias trail flowers all summer.
See Chapter 14.

**Bromeliads**
Many kinds. Easy to keep. Use in "trees" or in pots.
See Chapter 14.

**Calathea Makoyana**
Peacock-plant. Oval leaves. Alternately large and
small olive-covered ovals on a field of translucent,
pale yellow-green. One to 2 feet tall.

**Callisia Elegans**
Striped inch-plant. Leaves olive-green lined with
white stripes. Underneath, purple. Hugs the ground
or hangs over pot, showing purple undersides.

**Cephalocereus Senilis**
Old-man cactus. Slender, closely ribbed column
covered with long, gray hairs.

**Cyrtomium Falcatum**
Holly-fern. Leathery, shining, dark-green fronds.
Very durable.

**Davallia Fejeensis**
Rabbit's-foot fern. Brown, furry rhizomes give rise to
finely cut, graceful, and durable fronds.

**Echeveria Pulvinata**
Chenille-plant, plush-plant. Rosette of thick, fleshy,
green leaves with red edges, covered with silver-white
fur. Many other kinds.

### Echinopsis Multiplex
**Easter lily cactus.** Barrel-shaped. Dark green, close ribbed. Brown spines. Rosy flowers in late spring.

### Fittonia Argyroneura
**Mosaic-plant.** Dark, olive-green, oval leaves with a network of silver veins. Creeping habit.

### Gasteria Verrucosa
**Oxtongue-gasteria.** Succulent, fleshy, thick, pointed leaves. Deep green covered with raised white spots.

### Geogenanthus Undatus
**Seersucker-plant.** Quilted leaves are dark, metallic green with bands of pale gray. Red beneath. Compact and low-growing.

### Gynura Aurantiaca
**Velvet-plant.** Green leaves densely matted with violet or purple hairs. Purple veins. Iridescent. Purple-passion-vine has 2-foot-long stems which twine or hang. Both have tiny orange flowers.

### Haworthia Fasciata
**Zebra-haworthia.** Succulent, upward-curving leaves with warty growths on the backs. Terrarium plant.

### Hedera
**Ivy.** Many kinds, many uses.

### Kalanchoë
Some cover themselves with masses of bright-red flower clusters, others sport orange flowers. The panda-plant is a succulent form with soft, spoon-shaped leaves covered with dense white felt.

### Mammillaria Elongata
**Golden-stars.** Clusters of light-green cylinders covered with yellow spines. Good cactus for dish gardens.

### Maranta Leuconeura Kerchoveana
**Prayer-plant.** Grayish-green leaves with chocolate blotches turning green with age. Leaves become vertical in darkness, horizontal in light.

### Nephrolepis Exaltata Bostoniensis
**Boston fern.** Rich, green fronds spread gracefully to 3 feet. 'Fluffy Ruffles' is a dwarf variety with densely ruffled fronds. Whitmanii is lacy and open.

**Nicodemia**
Indoor-oak. Metallic-blue to green leaves are shaped like oak leaves. Shiny and iridescent.

**Notocactus Leninghausii**
Golden-ball-cactus. Close-ribbed cylinder covered with soft, golden hair. Yellow flowers, which are fragrant.

**Opuntia Microdasys**
Bunny-ears. Flat, fleshy, green cactus with neat rows of yellow-to-brown spine tufts. Young pads grow, earlike, at the tops of older ones.

**Pelargonium**
Geranium. Many kinds. See Chapter 14.

**Peperomia**
Many kinds, some with wrinkled leaves, some with leaves designed like watermelons, others with green leaves edged with cream. Low-growing, durable, and useful for terrariums or as table plants.

**Philodendron Oxycardium**
Also known as "cordatum." Tall, climbing vine with deep-green, heart-shaped leaves. Likes to ramble across tabletops and other surfaces. Trails nicely, too.

**Pilea Cadierei**
Aluminum-plant. Quilted foilage painted silver over vivid green to bluish-green. Panamiga has hairy, copper-colored leaves.

**Piper Crocatum**
Saffron-pepper. Green leaves with pink veins and purple undersides. It will climb on a stake or trail as a hanging basket.

**Polypodium Aureum**
Hare's-foot fern. Metallic, light-green fronds on wiry stalks. Furry, brown rhizomes look like rabbit's feet.

**Polystichum**
Holly-fern. Many kinds, some feathery, some stiff. *P. tsus-simense* good for terrariums.

**Pteris**
Brake-fern. Many kinds, some with lemon-green foliage, others with variegated silver-and-green fronds. All have unusual foliage.

Part Two

# Decorating
# with
# Plants

*Chamaedorea elegans* palms

# 3. The Living Room

Your living room can be just what its name implies—a home for living, growing things.

Plants are a lot like humans. They come in all sorts of different sizes and shapes and colors; they like much the same kind of environment that humans find most comfortable; their needs are quite humanlike, a little food and water and an occasional bath now and then keeps us all happy. And plants make good living companions . . . after all, we've been coexisting happily for millions of years.

The best way to begin a satisfying relationship with plants in your home is to spend some time with your own thoughts about your furniture, your present decorating scheme, and how far you want to go in changing things around in order to decorate most effectively with plants.

## Taking Stock

Stand in a corner of your living room, with a sketch pad and pencil, and do your best to illustrate the room completely with all its details. Draw the walls and windows and shade the walls receiving less light than the others. Draw each piece of furniture, being careful to put each item in its proper scale and relationship to the rest of your decor. Draw the draperies. Draw the rug. Draw the vases and knickknacks on the tables and chests, and the pictures on the walls. If you're not the world's greatest artist, so much the better. The real purpose of this exercise is to force you to work hard, literally to struggle, to see each and every piece of furniture and accessory item in terms of mass and shape and how it sits upon the floor or otherwise occupies space. As you draw, you'll be studying how the elements in your present decorating scheme relate to one another. And, importantly, you'll also be analyzing each piece of furniture in a rather critical and unemotional way. Hopefully, you'll be able to separate the nostalgic qualities from the architectural qualities and see each item objectively in terms of its artistic contribution to your decor.

After you've finished your sketch, you should have a much clearer idea of the practical, esthetic, and nostalgic value of each of the elements in your decorating scheme. Now you can assign a relative value to each piece of furniture, each picture on the wall, to the draperies and slipcovers and rugs, and to the accessory items. You now have good, sound, practical, and intellectual reasons for hanging on to an item or for eliminating it from your future plans.

Your next step is to work up those plans.

## Planning for Plants

Draw a floor plan of your living room, carefully measuring walls, window and door openings, and odd angles. Make the drawing large in scale, say one-half inch to the foot. Get some colored paper, and after carefully measuring each piece of furniture, cut out its scaled-down equivalent using the same scale of one-half inch to the foot (don't forget to include cutouts of new pieces of furniture which you intend to include). Next, cut circles from green paper to represent plants. Circles an inch and three-quarters in diameter will represent plants that fall in the "Tall" class—up to six feet tall and up to three and a half feet wide. Circles one inch in diameter will represent "Medium" plants—those with heights of up to three feet and widths up to two feet. Don't bother with cutouts for small plants at this point.

Place your scaled-down furniture and plant cutouts on your living-room floor plan and start pushing them around into interesting groupings. Now is the time to experiment with some wild notions.

Create a conversation grouping of couches and chairs in an unusual place and screen it with plants. Move everything away from the brightest window and see what can be placed elsewhere in order to make room for a permanent window planting. Design a planting in a corner with the idea in mind of adding some naturalistic elements such as boulders, a waterfall, some fish. Partition off the front-door entranceway with plants. Hide the dining room with a screen of green. Create a private foliage den where TV addicts can view to their hearts' content. Even get rid of all the furniture and start fresh with giant cushions and luxurious plants.

When you've hit on some combinations of plants and furniture that offer interesting possibilities, give some thought to present traffic patterns. How do people enter and leave the room? Is it necessary to cross the living room to get from the kitchen to the staircase? Keep in mind that established traffic patterns are tough habits to break, and that your body will want to dash directly, and in a straight line, from the kitchen to answer the front doorbell, long after your mind has accepted the fact that there is now a chair and a plant in the way. It is much better to keep traffic lanes open and to work your furniture and plant combinations around them.

### What Plants Go Where?

You've been pushing bits of colored paper around for hours now and have come up with some novel plant and furniture combinations. Now to select the right plants for your groupings.

The best way to begin making decisions on plant sizes and shapes is physically to move your furniture and accessories to their new locations. Now you can tell just what general plant size is called for in each position. Turn to Chapter 2, Plants at a Glance, where over one hundred plants are pictured and described. The plants are listed in three categories. Tall plants are those usually purchasable in heights of from three feet

on up to six feet and over. Medium plants include those specimens usually found ranging in height from one to three feet. Small plants are the candidates for table-top, windowsill, planter, or terrarium use and range in size from tiny to one foot in height.

If you've decided that you want, say, two tall plants to stand over there on either side of the breakfront, turn to the list of tall plants and see what there is to offer. As you look at the pictures, try to visualize the plants in position next to the breakfront. Does their shape complement the piece of furniture? Would the plant's interior visual shapes and pattern, the character and growth habit of leaves and stems inside the plant's outline, enhance or detract from the appearance of the breakfront? How do the color and texture of the leaves and bark relate to the texture, color, and patina of the piece of furniture?

At first you are going to say that almost any of the plants would look marvelous in your living room, and that most of them would be appropriate companions for your furniture. You'd be partly right, too, because all plants are beautiful in their way, and any plant is much better than no plant at all. But by paying some serious attention to the great variety of character and personality from plant to plant, you will be able to design some truly outstanding plant and furniture combinations, and that's what decorating with plants is all about.

### Choosing the Right Plants

Each one of the plants referred to in this book has a distinct characteristic which makes it a more appropriate choice for enhancing one decorating scheme than another; one example of furniture design than another. The philodendrons run to large, leathery leaves, for instance. Some of them have leaves with deeply cut indentations, giving the impression that someone has been busy with a pair of scissors. Others have smooth-edged leaves with lobed wings at their bases. All of the philodendrons could be said to have a massive, glossy, leathery, tropical character. Consequently you would be justified in looking among other plant families for a companion to a delicate Louis XIV porcelain figurine. A small polyscias, or ming-tree, would be the perfect foil for the figurine but would do very little for a grand piano or a heavy library table.

Let's look at the positive characteristics of some plants to understand better how they might best be used in your own decorating ideas.

*Ficus nitida* and *F. benjamina* look very much like deciduous trees that you would expect to find growing in northern climates. Their bark is a soft fawn color marked with tiny, lighter-colored bumps arranged in horizontal patterns. The leaves of these plants are oval and a bright lime-green. New leaves are produced almost continuously and are a vivid chartreuse, giving the tree a pleasing two-tone effect. I am reminded a little of birch trees when I look at them, although the resemblance is slight. Somehow they manage to conjure up images of trees whose names I've forgotten, but whose character remains in pleasant memory. The look of these ficus trees is clean, contemporary, lyrical, sculptural, and fresh. They can stand alone, as pieces of living sculpture, or in concert with furniture.

I associate these ficus trees with smoothly carved stone or wood; with classic modern furniture such as Charles Eames's leather and rosewood armchair and ottoman, the Parsons table, the Saarinen pedestal tables and chairs, and many of the Knoll designs. I see these plants accompanying paintings in the French Impressionist style, photographs of serene people or places, a simple glazed pottery vase containing one rose or six Japanese anemones.

The broad-leaved members of the ficus family—*F. lyrata*, the fiddle-leaf, and *F. elastica*, the rubber-plant—remind me unquestionably of the tropics. Their leaves are thick and glossy. *Ficus lyrata's* leaves are fiddle-shaped, prominently veined and huge, often reaching a length of fifteen inches and a width of ten. Both of these plants have specific personalities and can be used to excellent advantage if you give some thought to their physical characteristics and correctly team

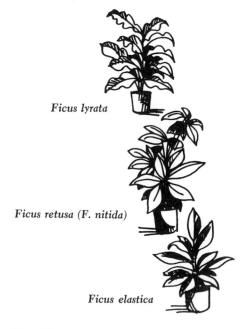

*Ficus lyrata*

*Ficus retusa (F. nitida)*

*Ficus elastica*

**Broad-leaved ficus varieties are tropical-looking.**

**The bold couch and plump cushions are complemented by this brave use of a specimen *Ficus elastica decora*. Note the interesting shadow patterns cast upon the wall and ceiling by the background plants. The more delicate foliage of these plants admits maximum light and balances the mass of the couch and rubber-plant.**

**Palms are graceful, elegant, sturdy and come in a variety of forms and shades of green.**

them up with the right piece of furniture. I picture *F. lyrata* with roughhewn stone sculpture or massive, bold wood carvings. A heavy, carved wooden chest can be wedded to a room containing otherwise more graceful and less massive furniture if its heaviness is lightened by a graceful fiddle-leaf fig.

Many varieties of palms have been cultivated for their beauty and value as indoor plants. The palms you buy at your greenhouse are really the seedlings and saplings of the huge and graceful trees so familiar in tropical climates. Generally speaking, they have single, unbranched trunks and may grow in clusters, as do the howea and chamaedorea palms, or they may grow singly, as do veitchia and phoenix palms. Usually their leaves are divided into many leaflets either in the shape of fans or feathers, with many long leaflets growing outward from a single, long, flexible stem. A point of interest—some palms are surprisingly hardy in other than tropical or subtropical climates. Northern California dwellers won't be surprised to hear that palms grow as far north as Portland and Seattle. But would you believe London, Edinburgh, and southern Russia?

In nature palms grow in solid stands and in the company of broad-leaved evergreen trees and shrubs. Keep this in mind when you group them with other plants indoors. They all tolerate shade and rhapis, chamaedorea, and howea seem to prefer it.

The tall, gracefully arching palms are best represented by the *Howea Forsteriana*, the kentia-palm of the florists. Its leaves are pinnate, which means that they are formed like a feather, with separate leaflets growing along the sides of a long, slender leaf stalk. Its graceful fronds grow successively larger and in nature they form a sixty-foot trunk (don't worry, they're slow growers). Howea's leaflets are a waxy deep-green and will remain so through surprisingly adverse conditions. Tall specimens could be used singly for an umbrella effect over a rattan armchair and reading table. Add a hanging Tiffany lampshade and you will create a most inviting Gauguinesque grouping (or Sydney Greenstreetesque, if you are an old detective-movie fan).

Howea and other palms have long been associated with Victoriana, probably because their adaptive and forgiving qualities made them the forerunners of the houseplant movement. A palm makes an excellent companion for a gleaming brass urn, a comfortable overstuffed chair, oak furniture such as a sideboard, a cupboard, or a cavernous rolltop desk. As a matter of fact, you don't have to throw away your old furniture and redecorate with authentic Victorian (or other period) pieces to capture the essential charm of the era. A choice piece of furniture or two, combined with the appropriate plants, can often capture the warmth and personality of the period while avoiding many of its negative aspects, such as its heavy brocade drapery, stiff, uncompromising settees and chairs, and its dark, rather foreboding atmosphere.

When I close my eyes and think very hard about houseplant-sized howea palms, I become aware of mental images that can be described by the words *stately, graceful, arching, protective, inviting, calm, elegant, masculine, sturdy,* and *eternal.* I picture them with subdued crimson, pure white, browns ranging from honey through rich chocolate; with leather, elegant woods, wicker, and precious, collected things. They make me think of books, serious ones on important subjects. I hear the music of Bach. Now you close your eyes and find out if you agree.

The philodendrons have been cultivated as houseplants almost as long as the palms. These tough and durable tropical dwellers fall into two main classes.

The arborescent, or treelike, philodendrons often reach heights of from six to eight feet in houseplant specimens. They develop large leaves and sturdy, self-supporting trunks. Use them for lush tropical effects, or individually as free-standing architectural statements, or as imposing silhouettes against a wall. *Philodendron Selloum* has dark-green, glossy leaves which are deeply cut, giving it its popular name, finger-leaf philodendron. *P. eichleri* is a magnificent specimen plant

Wicker and palms transform this room into a tropical verandah. Hanging fuchsias add color. Other plants are: rhipsalis (hanging near fuchsia), a 'Fluffy Ruffles' fern in the left foreground, a *Ficus benjamina* way in back, and several small potted palms.

Huge leaves of *Monstera deliciosa* (commonly called split-leaf-philodendron) seem to be reaching out for a drink of water.

40

with giant elephant-ear leaves often reaching four feet or more in length. You could build an entire decorating scheme around just one of these massive beauties.

The second main class of philodendron is the self-heading type. Familiar representatives include the split-leaf philodendron (which isn't a philodendron at all, but a monstera), *P. panduriforme*, the fiddle-leaf philodendron, and *P. oxycardium* (usually sold as *P. cordatum*, a different species), whose heart-shaped glossy-green leaves are seen tumbling out of pots and planters and heirloom mugs in so many houses across the country.

Any philodendron you see growing against a slab of wood or bark falls into the self-heading, or vining, class. In nature these plants shape themselves to the trunks of trees and cling by means of aerial roots. In your home, the slab of wood or bark takes the place of the tree not only by furnishing support, but by giving the plant's aerial roots a surface

Slabs of osmunda-fern are used as supports for climbing plants, such as self-heading philodendrons, and for airborne bromeliads and ferns. Water climbing plants by dribbling water down the slab.

to cling to, thus releasing what is thought to be a hormone which allows the plant to develop large, mature leaves. If you've seen one of these plants which has outgrown its wooden support, perhaps you've noticed that the nonsupported stems bear only small and immature-looking leaves. The aerial roots also supply the plant with oxygen and help to overcome poor drainage, so don't remove them.

The philodendrons are lush, large-leaved, tropical-looking jungle plants. Their leaves are thick, glossy, and deep green. In nature they grow beneath tall plants and trees and so are accustomed to reduced light. Their natural companionship with taller plants suggests a similar use for them in home decorating.

Small and medium-sized philodendrons can be used to "face down" tall plants. Let's say that you have designed a window planting, using tall *Ficus nitida* and palms to frame sun-loving, flowering plants. The philodendrons, with their less demanding light requirements will be quite happy to occupy the darker areas to either side of the window, in front of the tall plants, and toward the front of the window.

Small philodendron plants serve as an effective underplanting for a naturalized effect by suggesting the lushness of the thickly carpeted, tropical forest floor. Use small plants for tabletop plantings, too, particularly *P.* 'Lynette'. This one forms a rosette in the form of a bird's nest, with leathery fresh-green leaves patterned with deeply sunken veins that run from midrib to the edge of the leaf.

The most common and perhaps best loved of the philodendrons is *P. oxycardium* (or *cordatum*). It is extremely durable and can be made to perform some useful decorating tricks. Its thin stems and heart-shaped leaves will quickly cover an area if you will supply some moisture-retentive material, such as bark or fiber, to it for clinging purposes. In this way you can cover areas ranging in size from a foot square to an entire wall.

*P. oxycardium* will climb fast and high, too, if you will give it the support and guidance of wire or string. Train it to frame an entire window, or a painting, or a mirror. Or you can take advantage of its tendency to trail gracefully if left unsupported. Let clouds of it tumble from a high rafter. Or let it spill daintily over the edge of a table, chest, or bookcase.

Philodendrons make me think of the jungle; the tropical rain forest where moisture abounds and where sunlight is so filtered through layers upon layers of foliage that the floor of the forest is bathed in a soft green light. I think of heat and of rampant growth; of pale-green new leaves thrusting upward toward the light. I think of words such as *massive, powerful, wet, lush, green, growth, thick, shade, bold, tough, leathery, exotic.* You might include these plants if you want to make a bold, assertive statement in your home-decorating scheme. So use the philodendrons freely . . . but use them courageously and with definite purpose.

The dracaenas are members of the lily family, although the ones you'll see in the greenhouse bear no resemblance to the Easter variety. These plants are robust and durable and adjust well to low-light conditions. The dracaenas offer you a nice variety of plant forms, all of which have proven to be important and decorative houseplants.

*Dracaena marginata* bears a dense, terminal rosette of narrow, fifteen-inch-long, deep-olive leaves on long, slender trunks. In small to medium-sized plants, these trunks are straight. In tall sizes the trunks assume exotic shapes, bending and twisting almost as if they had been trained. Some branches seem to have bent sometime ago under the weight of their leaves, but now, finding new strength, are growing upward once more. Others appear to have satisfied a desire to grow sideways for a while, just to see if they could do it.

You can take advantage of D. *marginata*'s interesting growth habits by selecting one with just the right shape and teaming it up with a particular piece of furniture or art object. Let's say that you are leaning toward the Oriental influence in your decorating ideas. Many times these plants assume shapes suggestive of bonsai and of the windswept trees so often seen in Chinese and Japanese landscape paintings. And because the plant's leaves are borne in clusters at the end of long, slender stems, D. *marginata* has a light, airy look very much in keeping with the bold, yet delicately elegant Japanese look.

*Dracaena Massangeana* is sometimes called the corn-plant. You'll see why when you examine the arching bright-green leaves which have bands of light-green and yellow running down the center. The leaves are formed in rosettes and are borne on slender trunks, or canes. Greenhouses and florists offer these plants in pots which also contain *Philodendron oxycardium*. The philodendron climbs on the canes and eventually covers them completely. Left uncovered, D. *Massangeana*'s canes are strong and upright and bear their foliage proudly. Tall specimens are useful in confined areas because the leaves are out of the way of swinging knees and elbows, armloads of groceries, and kids on tricycles.

D. *Massangeana* makes a good background plant in naturalistic groupings. Its foliage is borne high and its bare stems make room for plants that like to spread. Seen in a setting such as this, D. *Massangeana* looks quite moist and tropical. But seen singly, and at a distance, it takes on another character and becomes very much like a palm tree, seen in nature and far away.

You can create an optical illusion and add a feeling of spaciousness to your living room by trading on D. *Massangeana*'s resemblance to distant palms. Clear everything away from the wall which is farthest away from you as you enter the room. Select plants with tall, straight stems and which bear foliage at the tips only. The heights of the plants should range from half the distance from floor to ceiling to three-quarters of the wall height. Group the plants together, side by side and in depth, so that the foliage occurs at an interesting variety of heights. Resist the temptation to hang anything at all on the wall. As a matter of fact, the wall should be painted a neutral, soft color or, preferably, white. Now, seen upon entering the room, the plants do indeed look like far-off palm trees. Their columns of vertical trunks add height to the room, and their apparent distance gives an optical illusion of greater depth.

There are more dracaenas that will be useful to you in your home. *D. Warneckii* offers stout, branching canes covered with sword-shaped, leathery leaves of a fresh green color, streaked milky-green in the center and bordered by a translucent white band on each side inside the narrow, bright-green edge. It's great for dark locations. *D. Sanderiana* gets by on little light, too, and is a neat little plant with elegantly twisted leaves, deep green, somewhat milky, with a band of white at the margins.

Ferns grow wild all over the world, yet they are quite civilized as house-guests. Most ferns offered for sale are selected from the tropical and subtropical varieties, and you should try to give them the moist-cool air and porous, woodsy soil they need to be completely happy. At the beginning of this century, before the advent of steam heat with its hot, dry air, there was hardly a home that didn't have a Boston fern or two growing contentedly in a room that was kept "on the cool side."

Ferns have been around for a long time. And for good reason! They make handsome and faithful houseplants, provided they are kept moist at the roots. Nephrolepis, better known as the Boston fern, has given birth to many new varieties such as *Whitmanii*, 'Fluffy Ruffles', and other feathery, bright-green examples. Cyrtomium is often called the holly-fern. It has dark-green, leathery, glossy leaves and an open, airy, almost palmlike habit. The remarkable adiantum ferns have thousands of leaflets borne on thin, almost invisible, wiry stems. They look like a cloud of glittering green coins. The lacy-leaved davallias have creeping rhizomes which look like rabbit's feet. *Asplenium Nidus*, the bird's-nest fern, has fresh-green, lacquered leaves arranged in rosettes. The weird-looking but friendly platycerium, or staghorn-fern, will make you famous in the neighborhood for your exotic taste. The tree-ferns—cyathea, cibotium, and dicksonia—grow tall and graceful and give you the opportunity really to use your imagination in designing a place for them.

If you have a nondrafty, north-light location in your living room, you can design an all-fern landscape. Be prepared to lower the temperature at night down to sixty, or even fifty-five, degrees, and to furnish your ferns with plenty of humidity.

You can build a tumbling stream with waterfall, or you can create a quiet setting with a still, calm pool, populated or fishless as you choose. The more moisture-laden air you can promise your ferns, the more daring you can be in their selection. Some ferns have fronds that contain a large percentage of water which must be maintained, or the ferns will collapse.

If you think that you can keep the relative humidity at 70 percent, or better, go ahead and experiment with the adiantums and the maidenhair-ferns and the delicate pteris varieties, some of which look like miniature tree-ferns. If you cannot keep the relative humidity high in the immediate neighborhood of your fern planting, be content to use the more durable and less demanding polypodiums, davallias, and cyrtomiums. Remember, though, that even the more durable ferns love their moisture and will respond to regular mistings with water. Don't let their feet get wet, though. As in all group plantings, a shallow tray filled with pebbles, with water up to the level of the pebbles, is highly recommended as a base for the plants. The potted ferns stand on the pebbles, thus allowing excess water to drain from the pots, and they benefit immensely from the evaporation of the water in the tray.

For ferns in the "Medium" height range, which are useful as a background planting for the small varieties mentioned above, ask your plant man to show you the *Cibotium Schiedei*, or Mexican tree-fern. It grows very slowly and is usually sold without trunk in eight- or nine-inch tubs. Its pale-green, showy fronds are very much in keeping with the tall dicksonias, other cibotiums, and cyatheas.

## Tropicals That Don't Look It

Perhaps you'd like to get away from the moist, tropical-looking plants and try a more "northerly" approach to your horticultural decorating. There are many plants which, although they grow in the hottest of climates, bear strong resemblances to trees and shrubs usually found in the colder regions.

*Araucaria excelsa* is an evergreen conifer which was discovered growing nobly in the forests of Norfolk Island, off the east coast of Australia. In its natural home it reaches heights up to 220 feet,

*Ficus benjamina*

*Araucaria excelsa*

**Ficus benjamina and Norfolk Island pine bear strong resemblance to northern trees, but are tropical.**

but you won't have any trouble locating one of these Norfolk Island pines in a size more suitable to the dimensions of your living room. Its fresh, green, formal, and elegant character is not at all diminished by its smaller stature. Consider creating a forest effect by using these pines in group plantings. Or use them in pairs to flank a piece of formal furniture.

*Ficus nitida* and *F. benjamina* have been mentioned previously as having the characteristics of northern trees. Polyscias (ming-tree), podocarpus, dizygotheca (aralia) all deserve to be included in this category. So do *Citrus mitis*, or calamondin orange (when it's not bearing oranges), crassula, Chinese jade, pittosporum, cypress, and *Ligustrum lucidum*, or privet.

Look at the pictures of the plants mentioned above, and see if you agree with my analysis of their character and personality. If you don't agree with me, fine. Whatever your own views are, it means that you are thinking of plants as elements of design. Now, as you are learning to sort out the vast number of plants offered for sale, in terms of their physical characteristics, you should begin to think about their living needs as well.

## What Plants Need to Keep Healthy

The most important factor to be considered in selecting the right plant for the right spot is proper light. You should spend some time observing where the sun hits in your room, and for how many hours a day. Draw a simple sketch showing the path of the sun and write in the number of hours of sunlight each area receives. Next, make a careful analysis of the amount of light available to areas not reached by direct sunlight. Chapter 13, under "Light," will tell you how to measure your light fairly accurately. Take readings of the amount of light received in every location of the room and indicate these amounts on your sketch.

Take these readings several times a day for at least a week. If you are in the middle of a rainy spell, or a particularly bright, clear one, you should wait until the unusual meteorological situation has passed. The idea, of course, is to get a week's worth of readings that will give you an accurate picture of the average amount of light a plant can expect to receive over an extended period of time. Check your readings every now and then, as the seasons progress. It's easy to make winter and summer adjustments in your plant locations to take advantage of the sun's changing position relative to your windows.

Next, try to determine the relative humidity of your living room (see Chapter 13, "Moisture"). Most tropical plants like high humidity and now is the time for you to decide whether or not you are going to want to take the trouble to keep them happy in their moisture requirements. If you've got air conditioning running constantly, or have the heat turned up most of the time, your air will be too dry to support most tropical plants. You can raise the humidity by grouping plants and placing their containers on trays of pebbles or gravel, kept almost full of water. If you have radiators, you can place pans of water on them, thus adding to the moisture content of the air. Spraying the leaves of your plants with water once or twice a day will help them a lot, too. But of course the best way to be successful with plants is to select the right plants in the first place. To choose "iffy" plants on the basis of a mental promise to bathe them daily and to leave pans of water scattered about is to place yourself in unnecessary thralldom to your plants—not the best condition for cohabitation among any living species.

Lastly, take note of the temperature variations to be expected in your living room over the course of the day and night. Many of your plant candidates will show a preference for a temperature range of from 65 to 80 degrees Fahrenheit. Those that prefer a warmer or cooler temperature should not be expected to be happy out of their range. Neither should the members of your family, so choose plants that will adapt to your way of life . . . not the other way around. You can drop the heat by about ten degrees at night after you go to bed, though. All plants need a period of relative coolness in order to convert starches, manufactured during the day, to soluble sugar.

## The Window Area

Plants placed directly in front of a window will of course receive the most light from that particular window. The direction in which the window faces and the obstructions outside the window determine the number of foot-candles of light the plant will receive.

Windows facing south will admit direct rays of the sun to all of the leaves of a plant for at least four hours of the day, providing that buildings or trees do not block the sky. A minimum of fifteen hundred foot-candles can be expected here.

Flowering plants will thrive in this location. Try the faithful geranium family, and amaryllis, gardenia, hibiscus, kalanchoë, and lampranthus. Easter lilies and spring-flowering bulbs such as narcissus, hyacinth, and tulip should be placed here until the flower buds show color. Then you should remove them from any direct sunlight in order to get the longest possible period of bloom. Citrus plants, such as the calamondin orange, thrive in sun. Crotons are not flowers but they do a flower's job with their ornamental leaves of every imaginable combination of reds, yellows, pinks, copper, maroon, and orange. Give them plenty of sun.

Always remember that the sun will draw water more quickly from plants placed directly in its rays, so don't let your sunny window garden become too dry.

If your window faces east or west, and is not blocked by trees or buildings, you should be getting about three hundred foot-candles of light for your plants. Incidentally, plants placed on either side of, or five feet away from, a south window will also receive this amount of light.

East or west is the best location for plants that require good light but will not tolerate direct sunlight for any appreci-

45

able length of time. Luckily the great majority of foliage plants, available from florists and greenhouses, will do well in this location. Araucaria, dizygotheca, the ficus varieties, podocarpus, polyscias, and yucca are just a few of the tall plants you might consider. You can have some flowering and fruiting plants here, too, if you are careful to choose the right ones. Try aphelandra, azalea, capsicum, chrysanthemums, cineraria, cyclamen, and other gift plants. Gloxinia, saintpaulia and other gesneriads, the many bromeliads, solanum, and all of the succulents, including cacti of all shapes and sizes, will do well at this exposure. So will many of the medium to small foliage plants such as pittosporum, euphorbia, and crassula, to name just a few.

An unobstructed northern exposure will yield your plants about 150 foot-candles of light. This is considered a medium light intensity. It is also available to plants placed to either side of, or five feet back from, an east or west window. Plants placed ten feet back from a south window will also receive medium light.

You are going to have to be happy with foliage plants at the north window, because there just isn't enough light available to maintain flowering plants (although if you don't insist that your flowering plants actually flower, some of them will grow nicely, as foliage plants, in a northern exposure).

The florist industry has long recognized the fact that low natural light, overheating, and dry air are the very conditions most likely to be found in houses throughout the country. Therefore a great many plants have been introduced over the years that have been tested under adverse conditions such as might be found in the home. Those that have proven their ability not only to survive, but actually to adapt to low light and humidity, are the ones offered for sale today.

The philodendrons offer many possibilities for low-light areas. Aglaonema, aspidistra, spathiphyllum, scindapsus, and syngonium are rock hardy. Palms offer several extremely valuable varieties to low-

light conditions: try howea (or kentia) or either of the chamaedoreas, the bamboo and *Neanthe bella* palms. The dracaenas are right in there braving the adverse light conditions, too. *Dracaena marginata* comes in many shapes and sizes, from full-foliaged small to medium-sized plants, to fantastically twisted long trunks topped by tufts of deep-green slender leaves. *D. Massangeana* caps its canes with sprays of bright-green leaves resembling those of the farmer's corn plants. *D. Warneckii, D. Rothiana,* and *D. Sanderiana* are useful, attractive, and need little light.

The ubiquitous sansevieria, or snake-plant, has been putting its tough, adaptive habits to work for over fifty years in homes all across the country.

And finally, many of the ferns, such as the davallias and the nephrolepis varieties, will reward you with generous arching fronds of green, despite the low-light conditions you ask them to put up with.

A low-light intensity of seventy-five foot-candles is all that can be expected from an obstructed north window. It is the amount of light plants will receive if placed to either side of, or five feet back from, a north window which is not blocked by outside structures or trees. Plants located to either side, or ten feet back from, an *obstructed* east or west window will receive low-light. So will plants placed ten feet back from, or a few feet to the side of, an east or west window with a clear view. Place plants several feet to the side of, or fifteen to twenty feet away from, a south window and the light intensity drops drastically to around seventy-five foot-candles.

If you have windows on one wall only, that wall will be the darkest one in the room. This can work to your advantage if you have a sunny southern exposure and want to develop a window planting that includes a wide range of plants including some that flower.

Put your flowering plants in front of the window, in the direct rays of the sun, and surround them with plants requiring good light, but not full sun. Place low-light tolerant plants to either side of the window, to act as a framing device for your display. Remember to rotate these flanking plants regularly so that all of their foliage receives an equal amount of light over a period of several days. Generally speaking, these flanking plants will require less water than the ones placed directly in the sun. Let the soil dry out to a depth of a couple of inches between waterings. Then water heavily, making sure the entire pot or container is saturated. Then allow to become dry to the touch again. Of course, the best way to be sure that you are treating your plants well is to check each plant's specific needs. You'll find the key to this information contained within the plant descriptions in Chapter 2, Plants at a Glance.

Hanging baskets act as draperies, aided by the sweeping fronds of the palms at either side of the window. Comfortable chair makes the planting a good place to hide in.

## Ways to Plant Your Window

A big picture window admits a lot of light, and if you are lucky enough to have one, you won't have to cluster all of your plants close to it—there should be enough foot-candles for all.

Try designing a green-bowered sitting area around your picture window. Use arching palms to frame the window (and to do away with the need for draperies). Hang baskets of ferns and cissus from the ceiling at various heights, keeping in mind that they will block some of the light that would be available to other plants in the room if the window area were left unobstructed. Complete the hideaway effect by tucking a comfortable chair in behind several free-standing *Ficus lyrata*, or fiddle-leaf fig, a couple of *Clusia rosea*, for low-level foliage effect, and a good-sized, well-shaped brassaia (better known as schefflera).

If your picture window is the only source of natural light, or if the view it offers is breathtaking, you won't be interested in this next idea. But if you've got additional windows in your living room, how about turning the entire picture-window area over to a fantastic, tropical jungle? Tree ferns can form a canopy over different varieties of dwarf-palms, dieffenbachia, and brassaia. These medium-

A. Stand plants on wooden boxes to vary typography. Featherock boulders hide boxes. Make streambed out of black builder's plastic and staple to boxes. Plants hide construction details.

B. Small submersible pump is hidden in lower pool, recycles water through tubing (hidden by foliage) to reservoir at back and top of planting. Set entire planting on heavy-duty builder's plastic so that you can water nonselectively. Watch out for pinhole rips, though, which can allow damaging seepage.

sized plants are set upon benches constructed of ordinary 2 x 4 lumber, in order to give the impression of different levels of topography to the planting. Small areca-palms, brassaia, *Clusia rosea* hide all evidence of man-made structure. Finally, the floor of this miniature rain forest is carpeted with marantas, rambling episcias, fatsia, and helxine, the tiny-leafed baby's-tears. A tiny mountain stream and musical waterfall were designed to wander among rock outcroppings and boulders. The rocks are real but extremely light, a fraction of the weight of a similar-sized ordinary rock. They are called featherock and can be found at your nursery or garden center.

Maybe your living room is too small to accommodate a full-scale jungle planting. Or perhaps you would prefer a more formal approach to your decorating scheme. Formal arrangements can be designed to include plants requiring the exact light conditions that your picture window offers. A pair of brassaia should do well in unobstructed east- or west-facing windows. So would a pair of large dizygotheca, or aralia; polyscias, or ming-tree; araucaria, or Norfolk Island pine; and others. For a window facing north, look into the philodendron family and consider some of the palms, like howea and *Chamaedorea erumpens*, the bamboo-palm. If you like the idea of having a planter behind the sofa, you'll have to adjust your selection of plants for it to the light admitted by the window. Remember that flowering plants will want that southern exposure because they need the direct sun. Saintpaulias and other gesneriads; cyclamen, and many of the other gift plants; and the bromeliads are some of

A. Plants march across the back of the couch, supported by unseen planter. Matched *Ficus nitida* trees frame the seating area. Off-center fern takes stiffness out of formal design.

B. Planter can be supported by orange crates or by fancy engineering. Make planter waterproof, add pebbles and water.

Hanging plants are all the "drapes" this room needs. They filter the light through their leaves and bathe the room in soft green.

**Stagger the heights of plants for added interest and to insure for each plant its fair share of illumination.**

the exceptions to the rule. Ferns of all kinds and several of the smaller philodendrons can be used in the planter when low light is to be expected.

Windows of less than picture-window dimensions are still important sources of natural light. If a small window faces south and admits direct sunlight, it will furnish as much illumination (if not more) to plants directly in front of it as a much larger window facing north. To my way of thinking, natural light is much more desirable, from a decorator's standpoint, than artificial light (the plants couldn't care less). So my advice is to play your windows for all they are worth, falling back on fluorescent lighting for your plants only when it is really necessary.

Nonurban dwellers can often find that their problem is too much direct sunlight. Fabrics can fade and leather upholstery can dry out and crack. Woods can become lighter-colored and their fin-

ishes can crackle and peel as a result of the sun's rays. Heavy draperies can be drawn during the brightest and hottest part of the day, but this makes the room dark and closed off. There is another way.

To help filter direct sunlight, and to bathe the room in a soft, green aura, hang trailing baskets of plants in front of the window. Now is your chance to grow masses of color. Geraniums, nasturtiums, lantana, rosemary, and cascade-petunias are just some of the trailing, sun-loving plants for you to choose from. Stagger the heights of the hanging plants and hang them in depth (away from the window). The further away from the window you get, the more you can use plants requiring less sun. Cissus, some of the ivies, hoya, tradescantia, and *Asparagus Sprengeri* are some of the possibilities. Properly hung, these clouds of bright color and vivid green will capture the sunlight before it reaches your furniture, but will admit soft illumination to the entire room.

When trees and shrubs are growing outside the window and can be clearly seen through it, it is possible visually to expand the apparent size of your living room by using just the right indoor plants for your window area.

Rhododendron is a popular outdoor foundation plant, and its broad, oval-shaped leaves are duplicated by the foliage of *Clusia rosea* and *Ficus elastica*. Leaves of forsythia and lilac seen through the window can be matched indoors by *Ficus nitida*. The taxus family has its visual counterpart in the podocarpus. Junipers, spruces, and pines can be effectively imitated by the *Araucaria excelsas*, or Norfolk Island pine. During the outdoor growing season, plant window boxes full of begonias, geraniums, and ivy. Do the same on the inside of the window. The effect we're after is to make the window something other than a hole in the wall. By making the window act as a bridge between the inside and outside worlds, it becomes a visual doorway, increasing the boundaries of your room to as far as the eye can see. The trouble with draperies is that they stop the eye at the wall and therefore delineate the architectural limits of the room.

Tropical plants that have the same characteristics (or as close as possible) as the plants growing outside of the window are used to hide the edges of the frame and to give the impression that the outdoor plants have marched right into the living room.

Incidentally, the wall opposite the window receives more light than the side walls or the window wall. It's a good location for plants, and if you are willing to go to some extra expense you can make it even better.

### It's All Done with Mirrors

Plants placed against mirrors receive more light because illumination is bounced back at them. Thus the plant receives a more uniform amount of light on all of its leaf surfaces than it would if it were standing against a nonreflecting surface.

Even if you are planning a modest planting away from a window, you should incorporate a mirror into your design. Mirrors can range in size and shape from the small, decorative kinds right on up to huge floor-to-ceiling jobs. Naturally, the greater the mirror area, the more light will be gathered and reflected.

Mirrors can play some very nice optical tricks that you can make work to your advantage. As you can see in the color picture which follows page 120, the room appears to have been doubled by the clever use of mirrors. The entire wall was covered with mirrors, but the individual sheets of glass (which ordinarily would make up a single, flat, reflective surface), were angled slightly so that it would be impossible for a person to see his own reflection in the glass, no matter where he was standing in the room. Next, a lush planting was designed and installed. Care was taken that the individual mirror surfaces should reflect plants . . . not furniture across the room. Joints, where the glass panels overlapped, were disguised by plants and so were the edges of the mirror. Even plants placed elsewhere in the room were carefully located so as to hide furniture, or to be reflected in the giant mirror.

The result is more than just a magnificent display of plants. The room has been made to appear much larger. In fact, one gets the impression that the entire wall is the entrance into a lush tropical conservatory.

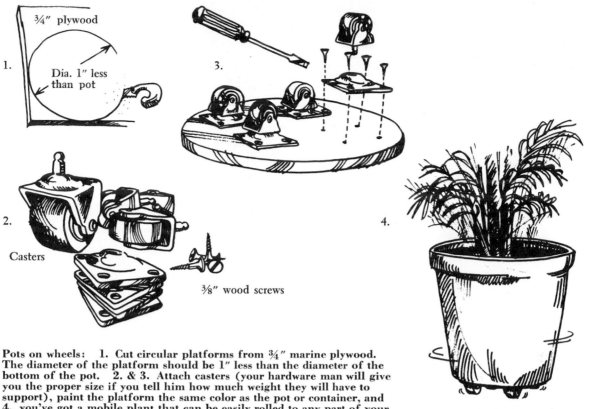

Pots on wheels: 1. Cut circular platforms from ¾" marine plywood. The diameter of the platform should be 1" less than the diameter of the bottom of the pot. 2. & 3. Attach casters (your hardware man will give you the proper size if you tell him how much weight they will have to support), paint the platform the same color as the pot or container, and 4., you've got a mobile plant that can be easily rolled to any part of your room.

Pot on wheels

Even a mirror of less heroic proportions can be made to play this optical trick. Simply angle it from the wall to a sufficient degree to make it impossible for anyone standing in front of the mirror to see his reflection in it. Then place plants of your choice in front and to either side of the mirror so as to border it nicely. Next, locate a tall plant or two at a point in the room where they will be reflected in the mirror. The result? The mirror becomes a window which overlooks a green, tropical outdoors.

So far we have discussed the window areas, and the wall opposite the window areas, and have identified them as the best locations for plants receiving only natural illumination. Next, let's see how we can take advantage of these locations without having to limit our plant groupings to them only.

### Plants on the Move

There is no reason why you have to design a static plant arrangement for your room. Your bright window or well-illuminated opposite wall can be rest-and-rehabilitation areas for plants which occasionally move into temporary locations in order to accommodate a special decorating scheme. In a few days they can be moved back to the beneficial and restorative environment of the well-illuminated areas.

Small to medium plants will be easy to move because their pots will not ordinarily be so large as to contain a heavy amount of soil. But tall plants are another matter. Put them on wheels (Figure 8).

The game of "musical plants" can be played every evening, if you wish, since there is no point in keeping plants next to a window if there is no light coming through it. Use plants to isolate the TV viewers from the readers and chatters. Roll plants into the dining room and make every meal a special occasion. Seal off a student stuck with homework from the rest of the world . . . and so on. Next morning, a few minutes' work sees all of the plants happily back at the window and the decks once again cleared for action.

A cloud of wax-plants hang suspended from the rafters in the living area of Roger Wohrle's greenhouse. The striking effect was only temporary since the plants were destined for market.

## Unusual Places for Plants

There are plenty of nooks and crannies in your living room which could be turned over to plants. These spots are likely to be out of the way of any meaningful amount of natural light, though, so we will be talking in terms of artificial light—fluorescent or incandescent.

As far as plants are concerned, light is light. For you, though, artificial light-ing is going to mean some extra work and expense. On the average, the trouble of installing fluorescent fixtures will fade into insignificance when you begin to realize how you can expand your deco-rating ideas by growing plants in unusual places.

The space underneath end tables, larger tables, and coffee tables, particularly the glass-topped kind, can become homes for plants. In the case of the glass-topped coffee table, the plants will have to receive all of their light through the glass, since there is no way to hide fluorescent fixtures under them. Fixtures can be easily and inexpensively concealed under the tops of the other tables, however, providing they have skirts or recessed areas behind which the light fixtures can be installed.

Fluorescent fixtures come in all sizes and are easily obtainable at your hardware or electric-supply store. The fixtures can be wedged in place tightly, with small blocks of wood. This does away with the necessity of using screws or nails and of marring valuable pieces of furniture. Run the cord down the leg of the table and then underneath as much rug and furniture as possible, until you reach an outlet. It's a good idea to run all of your artificial-light fixtures through one switch so that a flick of the finger turns everything on. If you've got to crawl around looking for a light switch, your plants are inevitably going to be forgotten now and then. Before you install the fluorescent fixture, line the underside of the tabletop with aluminum foil (you can glue it in place with easily removable rubber cement). The idea is to catch and reflect light, which would ordinarily be absorbed by the wood, and direct it back down at the plants. Keep this trick in mind when we get to other unusual locations for plants.

Ferns are good choices for under-the-table plantings, providing you can supply them with sufficient moisture. As always, the shallow tray filled with pebbles and water provides a humidity-yielding base for the pots to stand upon. Additional insurance against drying out will be provided by periodic spritzing with a fine mist of water. Some other plants to consider for this location are: spathiphyllum, small howea palms and other varieties of this family, several of the philodendrons (particularly *P. oxycardium*), and aglaonema, sansevieria, aspidistra, small *Dracaena marginata*, *D. Warneckii*, and *D. Sanderiana*.

A. Wedge tubes and fixtures out of sight under skirt of table. Run wire down leg.

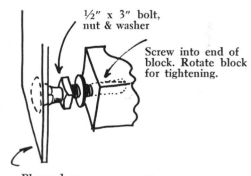

½″ x 3″ bolt, nut & washer

Screw into end of block. Rotate block for tightening.

Plywood or vinyl pressure plate against wall

B. Expandable gadget allows for nail-free installation of fluorescent fixtures under tables or against walls. Fixture is screwed to block of wood. Rotate block to push pressure plate against wall or table skirt, thus tightening fixture.

C. Remember to keep plants watered regularly. Water-pebble tray keeps humidity up, protects floor and rugs from spillage.

**A. Fireplace can harbor a single specimen plant or a lush grouping. Rotate plants to well-illuminated window area for occasional rejuvenations.**

**B. Install fluorescent tubing out of sight, up near the damper.**

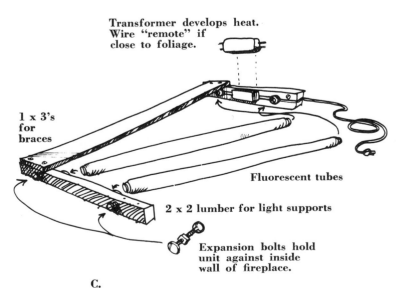

Transformer develops heat. Wire "remote" if close to foliage.

1 x 3's for braces

Fluorescent tubes

2 x 2 lumber for light supports

Expansion bolts hold unit against inside wall of fireplace.

C.

Do you have a fireplace in your living room? Why not turn it into a warm-weather greenhouse? Let it shelter a single magnificient fern, either hanging or free-standing. Place small plants within it at different levels. Or build in a miniature landscape. All you have to do for light is to place a fluorescent fixture up out of sight, near the damper. Just remember to vacuum out the area before you go poking around up there or you'll get an eyeful of soot.

Now for the bookcase. Weed out those books you never got around to reading, and never will, to make room for some plants. Build a terrarium right in between some favorite books and illuminate it artificially. Terrariums are really miniature conservatories. High humidity is maintained within the container because water vapor evaporating from the soil, and transpiring from the leaves of the plants, condenses upon the glass and is retained within the enclosure. Terrariums planted in demijohns, or other bulbous bottles with narrow necks, can go without attention for months at a time. Plantings in rectangular glass enclosures that have a much larger opening lose more water vapor, so you'll be giving the plants a fine misting with water every month or so.

For your terrarium container, use a fish aquarium. You should be able to find one that is just the right size, and many of the new ones have fused-glass corners which do away with the traditional steel bracing. Plant your terrarium with a landscape right out of some remembered childhood adventure. Use twigs and rocks and moss. Create tiny cliffs and caves and shop around for the perfect specimens of tiny ferns, marantas, and orchids.

While you're at it, buy two aquariums, one for the plants and one for some fish. Set the tanks on the same shelf, separated by books. Be as creative in designing the underwater seascape as you were in putting together the terrarium, and select fish with colorings that will complement or echo the colors of some favorite nearby accessory item.

Convert an old fish aquarium into a terrestrial landscape. Marantas, gesneriads, and orchids live comfortably with delicate pteris, adiantum, and polypodium ferns. Tiny outcroppings of rock and moss-covered twigs invite you to come down into this green world and explore. The terrarium is set above a tray filled with damp vermiculite, which keeps the air laden with moisture. Light is furnished by five cool-white, 20-watt fluorescent tubes plus four 10-watt incandescent bulbs.

Fishtank, before and after: Soften the hard edges by placing plants in front, to the sides, even on top. Try to find foliage plants which resemble their aquatic cousins inside the aquarium.

This desert landscape consists of cacti and other succulents. Arrange plants among outcroppings of rock and pieces of weathered wood. Add personal touches. Desertscape is contained in a 2-inch-deep tray. Plants are watered about every other week.

Perhaps your taste in reading runs to scholarly works, and you want to keep your bookcase planting as dry as your books. Enter the cacti. Cacti, and other succulents such as the euphorbias, the aloes, and the crassulas, thrive on very little water and adapt readily to artificial light. Use these plants in combination with sand, various-colored pebbles, rocks, pieces of driftwood, petrified wood, and so on.

The Japanese art of bonsai offers a possible treatment for your bookcase plantings. Bonsai, which means "tray planting," usually involves a single plant which has been trained within very small size limits and is growing in a controlled relationship with a rock, a piece of driftwood, or a mossy mound. Entire books are devoted to the creating of bonsai, and some good ones are listed in the bibliography at the back of this book.

Fortunately, for those of us who are not interested in spending years training a plant for our bookcases, ready-made bonsai is now available at most florists' or garden-supply centers. If your store doesn't carry bonsai, perhaps the dealer will consult his trade publications and tell you where you can find them.

There is a variation on bonsai called saikei. This word refers to the art of

In this miniature saikei world, several cypress trees, some rocks, moss, and sand have been assembled into a tiny, living environment. The major tree, in the foreground, seems to be growing from a cleft in the jagged rock. The plants receive their light from spotlights recessed in the ceiling. A larger bookcase would allow for the installation of fluorescent tubing which could be operated by an electric timer. Illumination for at least sixteen hours a day would be required.

"trayscape," the use of living plants in a beautifully designed and balanced miniature landscape. Traditional Japanese saikei methods call for the dwarfing and training of trees, just as bonsai does, but you should be able to find small plants that will give you an immediate effect. Purists are advised, again, to get one of the excellent books on bonsai and saikei. The Japanese attitude toward design and

Living room: A few specimen plants do the work of many and
are a lot easier to care for. The yucca and the piano work
well together because each is bold in outline, yet fine in
detail. At the right is a good example of a beaucarnea, or
pony-tail.

Dining room: No meal could be ordinary when
it is served in the dining room of architect
Warren Platner's Connecticut house. The
greenhouse is really an oversized bay window
but is large enough to accommodate a lush
array of tropical plants.

Living room: Architects Stanley and Laurie Maurer grouped
palms, schefflera, dracaena, and several small plants together
to separate their living and dining areas without diminishing
the feeling of space. The grouping stands on pebbles in a tray
kept filled with water for added humidity. Trailing plants
invite you to come on up.

**Kitchen:** This New York brownstone kitchen surrounds you
with easy-to-care-for spider plants, prayer plants, hoya,
wandering Jew, and shade-tolerant palms. Fluorescent lighting,
hidden by woodwork, keeps African violets colorful.

scale has valuable application to your decorating ideas, even beyond the use of plants.

To create a very personal, and unorthodox, saikei, gather together all of those sentimental mementos and knick-knacks you've collecting over the years and see which of them would lend themselves to your saikei planting. Create a forest of living minature trees and carpet its floor with pearls and diamonds and rubies and other bits of costume jewelry. Place a tarnished, miniature Statue of Liberty on a mossy hilltop. Paste passport-sized photos of members of the family on rocks and plant tiny trees among them. March antique lead soldiers across a mossy plain toward a dark and mysterious woodland. Resurrect childhood toy trains, their electrical innards forever short-circuited, and direct their tracks through the virgin forests and ocean shores of your saikei tray landscape.

Both bonsai and saikei will require artificial light, and if you are growing actual dwarfed trees their light requirements will be different from those of your tropical houseplants. The subject is covered in Chapter 13 under "Light." Special considerations as to soil, watering, feeding, and insect control are also covered in Chapter 13.

A bit of carpentry can turn a floor-to-ceiling bookcase into a showcase for bromeliads while you still retain its usefulness as a bookcase. Bromeliads are exotic plants which grow in the crotches of tree branches in the tropical forest. They get all of their nourishment from the air, catching and storing water in the cups formed by their tight rosettes of leaves. You can duplicate their natural conditions by providing an interesting piece of driftwood for them to grow on. Drill holes in the wood large enough to receive the roots of your bromeliads after they have been wrapped in sphagnum moss or orchid fiber (osmunda).

Many bromeliads will stand a temperature variation from near-freezing to high. Your home temperature should be just about right. They do like filtered sun, though, so your artificial illumination

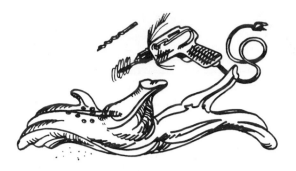

**A. Drill closely spaced holes in interesting piece of driftwood. Chisel out remaining wood between holes to create pocket large enough to hold bromeliad roots.**

**B. Wrap roots in sphagnum moss and insert in hole. Wire in place, if necessary. Remember to keep plant's cup filled with water.**

**C. Large bromeliad tree is constructed in same way as smaller version. Plants at base hide supports for tree. Tray holds pebbles and water for constant humidity.**

must be sufficient to supply good light. Long fluorescent tubes on either side of your bromeliad tree, as well as across the top of the recess, would be a good idea. The tubing can be hidden behind wooden extensions.

Hanging-basket plants can add a free and airy dimension to your decorating scheme. Use them as room dividers or space definers in the same way as you would use tall potted plants. Hang them at different levels from the ceiling right on down to the floor.

You can keep the containers and hanging wires simple and unobtrusive, or you can let your imagination really run wild in decorating them in bright and remarkable ways. Try using earthy terracotta pots hung from rawhide leather slings. Decorate the pots with your own designs or paint them in vivid primary colors or in different values of the same hue (use enamel; flat paint will peel). Encrust the pots with fake jewels, Christmas sparkles, or tiny multicolored Christmas balls. Paste pictures cut from magazines in collages on the pots. Wrap them in black-and-white blowups or photostats of favorite family photos. Throw a party and paste on funny portraits of all the guests. Hang your pots from ropes of fake pearls, diamonds, and emeralds. Braid hanks of bright yarn with contrasting tufts. Or weave thick ropes of natural, unbleached wool for your suspension system. Use heavy brass chains or slim, clear plastic rods.

If you can find glass globes with openings at the top and bottom, you can plant them and use them as hanging terrariums. I have several of these plant globes which are eighteen inches in diameter. They didn't come with holes at both ends (they were fishbowls, if you want to know the truth), so I had a glazier cut a five-inch-diameter hole in the bottom of each. Then I attached a six-inch-long eyebolt to the center drainage hole of an ordinary, plastic, six-inch-wide flower pot. I used a nut and a rubber washer on the inside of the pot, and one each on the outside (when tightened together, they made a waterproof con-

nection). Next, I attached a length of slender, stainless-steel, braided wire and passed it through the globe. The pot was then planted with dieffenbachia and spathiphyllum and pulled up snugly to the globe by the wire. After the wire was attached to the ceiling and the globe was hanging at the proper height, I disguised the plastic flowerpot by covering it with a small woven-reed basket. You can find these baskets at your friendly Japanese novelty store—or think up something even more attractive—to hide the ugly plastic pot. There is one last important touch to your hanging terrarium: A small X-shaped brace of wood spanning the top opening of the glass globe will insure good balance and proper location of the suspending wire through the hole.

An equally beautiful and less troublesome use of glass globes is to place the potting soil right inside the globe where it can be seen. Suspend the globe with strands of strong, transparent, fishing-line leader which crosses under the globe and is held in place with transparent reinforcing tape.

The appearance of the soil is just as important as that of the plants in these hanging terrariums, so make sure that it is dark, rich, and organic-looking. The Cornell mix described on page 147 will give you just the right effect. Fill the globe one quarter full with soil mix. Now add your plants. Choose those with interesting leaf shapes and colors. You'll be looking at them at eye level and from underneath, so look for plants with attractive colors, markings, and textures on the undersides of the leaves.

Of the ferns, the adiantums, the davallias, and *Asplenium Nidus* would all be spectacular. Spathiphyllum, aglaonema, aspidistra, and dieffenbachia offer you nice leaf textures and markings. Use the traditional terrarium plants—peperomia, haworthia, euonymus, ivy, and cryptanthus—in combination with taller plants. Or plant some globes with miniature terrarium landscapes, and others with lush, large-leaved, foliage plants.

Since the globes retain and recycle moisture and maintain a high relative

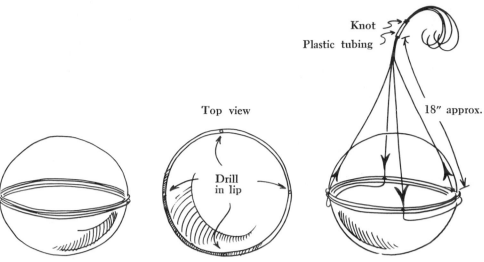

Knot

Plastic tubing

Top view

Drill
in lip

18" approx.

1.

2.

3.

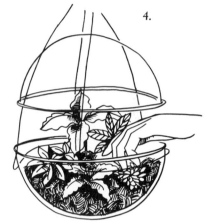

4.

A. Plastic hemispheres, which are found in plastic-supply houses, can be joined together to form a hanging terrarium.   1. Place the two halves together so that the lips line up.   2. Drill holes through both lips at 12 o'clock, 3 o'clock, 6 o'clock, and 9 o'clock.   3. Cut two lengths of 30-pound-test nylon fishing leader twice as long as the length required to hang the globe at the right height. Add a foot to each end for good measure. Pass a length of leader down through one hole and up through the hole next to it. Repeat for the two other holes. Cut a piece of clear plastic tubing about ½" long and pass the ends of the leader through it. Knot the leader 18" above the globe and on the top end of the plastic tubing (after leveling the globe so that it hangs plumb).   4. Raise the top hemisphere, plant the bottom section, water, drop the top down, hang, step back, and admire.

B. Hang a variety of globes at different heights for a room divider. Artificial lighting adds drama and needed illumination.

In this house you come inside to go outside. Light and sun flood the interior, glass-roofed patio, so native and tropical plants can coexist. Stakes support newly planted trees and flowers until they become established.

humidity, your plantings will require no attention for months at a time. You will have to do some occasional pruning, though, just to keep the plants inside the globes where they belong. Use a razor blade attached to a long dowel, and pick out the fallen leaves and stems with kitchen tongs or long tweezers made from knitting needles.

Artificial illumination for these hanging terrariums should come from incandescent floodlights or spotlights. There are some recent introductions by manufacturers of cool-beam spotlights which direct heat rays backward so that the light reaching the plant is relatively cool. A nice plus to using spots and floods is that their light is reflected from the glass globes in sparkling fragments.

## New Construction

If you've got plans to build a new house, or are in the process of building one right now, you can ask your building contractor to include a few small and inexpensive additions to the construction that will allow you greater freedom later on when you begin to decorate with plants.

Try to think ahead to when the house is finished, and decide whether or not you're going to have a mass planting in the living room (or any other room, for that matter). If the answer is yes, ask your builder's advice on how best to give additional support to the floor area upon which the plants will stand. He'll probably add bridging to the floor joists, at the very least, and if he thinks that you know what you are talking about he'll build extra beams under the area and support them with additional posts. You can also recess the planting area down into the floor at this time, with very little extra trouble and money. Also have your contractor drill a hole up through the floor close to the wall, and install copper tubing which should run either to a drain in the basement or to the outside of the foundation. This detail will save you much work when you want to drain the water from your planter tray. Make the tubing big enough so that bits of organic matter may pass through without stopping it up. Add a petcock to open and close the drain, and keep the drain clean by stopping it with a rubber plug.

Locate the areas of the ceiling from which you are likely to suspend hanging baskets or glass-globe plantings. The builder can easily nail 2 x 6 boards between the second-floor joists, giving you an expanse of solid wood in which to screw eyebolt supports for the hanging items. There's nothing worse than to drive a nail or screw through your finished ceiling or wall, in the hope of hitting a joist or stud, and finding nothing but thin air.

During construction is the time to anticipate your artificial-lighting needs for your plants. Talk your ideas over with your builder or architect, explaining the necessity of giving plants sufficient light when they are too far from natural light sources.

Incandescent spotlight and flood-light fixtures can be recessed into the ceiling and can later be directed at tall plants placed here and there in the room. Floor-to-ceiling fluorescent fixtures can be recessed into the walls for illumination of permanent planting areas. When they're not being used, the tubing can be hidden by a hinged section of wall, by a sliding partition, or by a removable hatch held in place by magnetic catches.

Sufficient wiring can be installed during construction so that you need never resort to ugly extension cords and the resulting overloading of circuits.

**Unfinished room. Some people can't wait to begin decorating with plants.**

Large window allows for vast planting. Tall plants filter light for smaller, shade-tolerant plants. If there is a basement below, floor must be braced to carry weight.

You can make sure that your special lighting is operated by switches that are independent of those controlling the ordinary house lighting. This is important, because you might want to install timers that will operate your plant illumination fixtures according to special needs of your plants. And if you are away from the house over a weekend, you might want to leave the plant lights on, right around the clock, for those few days.

How about enlarging your window area, as long as you're in the construction stage? Your builder can show you examples of bows and bays from the catalogs of various manufacturers. The extra money involved will be less than if you decide to install a special window later, and the opportunity such a window offers for the growing of plants will make you glad you decided to put one in.

*Dicksonia squarrosa*

# 4. The Dining Room

If you've got a permanent dining room, one that doesn't have to double as a living room during nonmealtime hours, it probably isn't subject to much traffic except when soup's on. Plants that you might elsewhere hesitate to place in the path of a hurtling ten-year-old can live safely here. Palms, for instance, often take up more than their share of space in a room that contains much activity, and there's a good chance that sooner or later their fronds will become damaged. But in the dining room, they can stretch out to their heart's content.

As you think about plants which might be appropriate for your dining room, consider the special character of this room and the role plants can play in helping to create a friendly and relaxed atmosphere during that most significant family get-together, dinner. Plants should be soft and serene in form. Their presence shouldn't intrude upon the family gathering or demand undue attention. During dinner the spotlight is on the meal, and all decorating devices—furniture and plants alike—should quietly complement the serving and enjoying of good food.

Palms have been favorite dining companions for years. Restaurants often use them, not only because of their durability and tolerance for low light levels, but because their feathery and graceful presence lends elegance to any menu. They'll do the same for you. Bamboo, areca, and *Neanthe bella* palms tend to

**Plants needed here! Young Jim Lebenthal agrees.**

A small plant-filled alcove invites you to dinner in style. Natural illumination from the skylight is sufficient for the low-light tolerant palms, dracaena, bromeliads, and hanging plants.

grow more upright and are good choices for dining rooms where space is at a premium. The more spreading kentia-palm needs more room but is rewarding because of its tolerance for low light.

Ferns give much the same effect as the palms but are much smaller. The Boston fern and some of its densely fluffy offspring make good centerpieces. Large specimens can be placed upon pedestals or used in hanging baskets. If you've got the right exposure at your dining-room window, baskets of ferns will make a beautiful and effective screen, but watch out that you don't block the light needed by other plants in the room. Bird's-nest ferns have unusually broad and unfern-like leaves which grow in rosettes. Not only do bird's nest ferns make good centerpieces, but they are also particularly useful because of their modest light requirements.

Gazebo effect can be expanded to cover other walls and can arch over and cover ceiling if height is sufficient. Back lattice with translucent plastic and illuminate from behind, for indoor-outdoor effect.

How about creating the effect of an outdoor gazebo? Tall *Ficus nitida* or *F. benjamina* trees will give the bowerlike effect you're looking for. You can even go all the way and tack up wooden lattice strips on the walls and ceiling, in graceful, arching patterns. If space is left between latticework and walls, lighting can be installed to give the effect of outdoor light coming through. Hanging baskets of ferns and medium-sized palms complete the effect.

Personally, I don't think that the more leathery-leaved and tropical-looking plants are appropriate for the dining room. *Ficus elastica*, the rubber-tree, and its cousin the fiddle-leaf fig are too fleshy-looking and their presence is somewhat overbearing for a room in which peaceful relaxation is the keynote. The philodendrons are also rather too aggressive for this room. I can picture a cutleaf philodendron creeping up behind me at the dinner table and demanding a hunk of roast beef.

Inviting further disagreement, I think that most forms of cactus are too prickly and bulbous for the average din-

ing room. *Dracaena marginata* and yucca are too spiky and the former has the additional disadvantage, in the context of the dining room, of appearing tortuous and convoluted. *Dracaena Massangeana* is quite another story. Its foliage is like leaves of corn and the plant itself is airy, tall, and palmlike. *D. Warneckii* and some of the other small- to medium-sized dracaenas will work well, too, and aren't particularly fussy about bright light.

### The Illusion of Space

Any small room can be made to appear larger than it really is through the use of visual tricks and well-chosen and cleverly placed plants. Large floor-to-ceiling mirrors can almost double the apparent size of the room. A mirror of this size becomes a doorway into what appears to be another room. The trick of creating the illusion of an adjoining room lies in making the reflection in the mirror seem to be different from the actual room which the eye perceives (though when the viewer stands before the mirror and sees his own reflection, the illusion ceases to exist). By

Graceful palms, dracaena, schefflera, and ficus separate dining area from living room without decreasing feeling of space. Water-pebble tray maintains humidity.

angling the mirror away from the wall, you cause it to reflect a part of the room other than where the viewer is located. Then, by massing plants in that part of the room, you allow the mirror to reflect them. People at a fixed position, say the dining-room table, see what appears to be an adjoining plant-filled conservatory. Tall plants at either side of the mirror hide its edges and further the illusion of space. There is more on mirrors in Chapter 3, The Living Room.

In Colonial days, wealthy merchants and businessmen were able to import elegant hand-painted or hand-blocked scenic wallpaper for their homes. Often the din-

ing room received this precious cargo, probably because the formal dining rooms of the day were kept closed off except for special occasions, thus assuring the protection of the valuable wallpaper. The scenes often depicted exotic landscapes and themes from Homeric legends. Despite the sometimes less than representational styles of these wall treatments, and the fact that the scenes were abruptly defined by wainscoting, doors, windows, tall furniture, and draperies, they served to expand the apparent size of the room enormously. The same trick can be used today in your dining room and not necessarily by using an expensive wallpaper.

### Turn a Wall into Mount Fuji

If you are very brave and moderately artistic you can paint an outdoor scene directly on a wall in your dining room. If you design it properly, the painting can appear as a view through an expanse of glass, or doorway, or a window.

Select a wall which is least encumbered by windows and doorways and paint the entire wall, or the section which you intend to design, a flat white, so that colors applied to it will be their most brilliant. Select your subject matter by clipping magazines and leafing through your old photo albums. Select a scene that you feel is within the range of your artistic capabilities, and do a few practice sketches in color to get the hang of it. You can also experiment with some alterations in design, putting in foreground trees and foliage. This last step is important because you're going to be matching this painted foliage later with real, live plants which will flank your wall painting and serve as a visual bridge into it. If, for instance, you decide to paint a distant, snow-capped Mount Fuji as seen from a lushly planted terrace, you would include foreground plants (perhaps *Ficus benjamina*, podocarpus, ming-trees, or schefflera, faced with smaller plants such as pittosporum, dieffenbachia, and fatshedera) which you would later match from the plant market.

Divide your completed drawing into identical squares by drawing equally spaced vertical and horizontal lines. Draw similar lines on the wall, with chalk, which are in proportion to those on the sketch. Now transfer the drawing to the wall. If your scene is on a color slide, project it directly onto the wall and trace it off. When you're ready to paint, get yourself some good brushes and casein or acrylic paints from your art-supply store. Caseins and acrylics dry quickly, come in brilliant colors, and can be applied without a diploma from an art school. Ask the art-store man for his advice on "fixing" the finished painting. There are clear fixatives which come in aerosol cans and which should do the trick. The last step

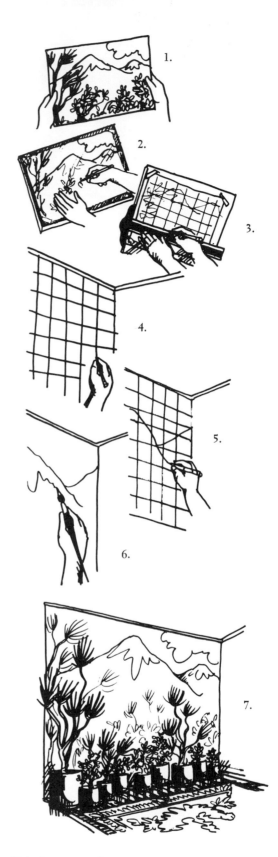

Painting a mural.
1. Select picture for transfer to wall.
2. Trace, eliminating all small and minute details.
3. Divide the tracing into squares.
4. Chalk larger-scale squares on wall.
5. Transfer drawing.
6. Paint.
7. Add plants which reflect the character of the plants in your painting.

is to place your plants on either side and in front of the painting, and stand back and admire.

A quick, less demanding, and ever-changing adaptation of the above idea is to project slides upon the wall during dinner. You can buy slides of exotic vistas or you can use your own. Here again let plants frame the wall area upon which the slides will be projected. Slides are particularly appropriate for showing at dinnertime, when they may furnish the only illumination in the room. You'll have to experiment a bit to find the best place to locate the projector so that people's heads don't appear in the beam of light. Try using mirrors to bend the light around tight corners. Try rear-screen projection, too, by stretching a sheet over a doorway and projecting on it from the other room.

### Tables and Settings

Flowering plants are especially nice for the dining-room table, but consider your choice of colors carefully. Advertising research tells us that the color blue is unappetizing (now you know why there are no blue M&Ms). If this information is correct, brilliant fuchsias and purples are out of place, too. Pinks and reds and oranges and yellows are all fine since these are the colors of most natural foods, along with green. A small, fruit-laden citrus surrounded with ivy makes a beautiful centerpiece. Foliage plants are appropriate for this place of honor, too, but select those with small or finely cut foliage. The jade-plant is succulent-looking, with plump stems and branches and glossy, thick leaves. Pittosporum and euonymus have small deep-green leaves and neat, light-colored stems and branches. Try hanging droplets of clear glass beads from the branches, to bounce back sparkles of candlelight.

When china is displayed on the shelves of a cupboard, try to find small plants that will echo the motif of the china. Often patterns are designed from a floral model which can be complemented by geraniums or other flowering

Mirror reflects scene (in reverse) on appropriate wall. Projector is hidden by plants.

plants. A twining-ivy pattern on china, and on silver too, can be matched by using needlepoint-ivy or even *Philodendron cordatum*.

### Special Occasions

Use plants to decorate your table in the mood of festive holidays. An obvious choice for the Christmas table is the Norfolk Island pine. Place a medium-sized specimen, complete with miniature decorations, in the center of the table, and small plants, as gifts, at each place setting.

Palm Sunday calls for tiny palms in three-inch pots at each plate, with a larger one in the center of the table.

The foliage of *Dracaena marginata* is lilylike and can be used in concert with Easter lilies at the Easter Sunday dinner table. If you find the fragrance of Easter lilies rather too heady for the confines of the dining room, use spathiphyllum instead for the same effect.

Thanksgiving dinners want masses of chysanthemums, geraniums, orange- and rust-colored coleus. Crotons often have the coloring of fall leaves and you should be able to select some brilliant, earthy specimens from your plant market. Use them with bright yellow mums and give them out to the guests as take-home gifts.

An ordinary run-of-the-mill dinner becomes a special occasion when you supply fresh, growing herbs at each place setting. Give everyone his own tiny pot of chives, for example, and watch baked potatoes with sour cream and chives take on new meaning. Parsley, mint, dill, sweet marjoram, and others can be served in the same way.

For kids' parties, build a miniature landscape for the centerpiece. You can use roasting pans for the waterproof containers, or you can build a light wooden frame and staple builder's plastic to it. Add rocks for mountains, mirror glass (or real water) for lakes and streams, moss for prairies, golden sand for beaches, and tiny plants for the forests. Place a little gift for each somewhere in the landscape and let each child come up, in turn, and remove his present. Or place little toy figures within the landscape and tag each one with a guest's name. Surround the entire framework for the planting with masses of bright flowers and ivy.

**Hide a gift for each child in the landscape and let each find his own.**

coleus

# 5. The Kitchen

In the good old preurban days almost every kitchen had its own garden just outside the back door. But these days there aren't many of us left who can still reach out into the garden and harvest a fresh armload of corn and tomatoes for dinner. The Industrial Revolution hasn't won completely, though. Your kitchen and a surprising number of other spots can be your garden and your harvest can be a cup of crisp, moist chives, fragrant nips of oregano, thyme, basil, tarragon, and other herbs, a bowlful of tender nasturtiums for salad.

## The Kitchen Window

Your agrarian-reform program begins right in your kitchen window. Most homes have at least one window placed right over the sink, and if ample light is available, plants grown here will receive both light and high humidity, a bonus.

Grow herbs of all kinds in the bright window. Plants grown for their fragrance, such as the spicy geraniums, are good, too. Grow experimental plants which you've produced from seed and cuttings taken from grocery-store vegetables and fruits. Grow any plant that has a taste or a fragrance. Plants that have neither are fine for other parts of the house, but for the kitchen, stick to plants that have some culinary attribute. After all, the kitchen is where delicious tastes and fragrances are concocted and your plants should do their part to promote good appetite.

If your windows are double hung (the kind that go up and down) or casement (the kind that open outward), shelving across the window will increase your garden area. In this case, glass shelving is better than wood because it allows for the passage of light to plants on lower shelves. Hanging baskets can be planted as miniature herb gardens and can be used with shelves, or by themselves. Make sure you've got the headroom, though.

If you are remodeling your kitchen, or are a really enthusiastic indoor gardener, consider adding on a bow or bay window in place of your present flat, double-hung or casement variety. With a bow or bay you can create a kitchen garden that will furnish you with an abundance of edibles and flowers. Bows and bays can be built from scratch by a person who is knowledgeable in carpentry, or can be ordered in a large selection of shapes and sizes from window manufacturers. Your local lumber or building-materials dealer can show you catalogs picturing the kinds available. He can supply you with your needs if you decide to do it yourself, or he can recommend a good carpenter who can handle the installation for you.

If you are willing to go through the time and expense of having your old window removed and a new one installed, you might consider going a bit further and installing a window greenhouse.

A bay window in back of the kitchen sink offers excellent light and humidity conditions to herbs, vegetables, and flowering plants. A "Tom Thumb" tomato climbs up the window, its fruits ripe and ready for the plucking. Taller rosemary and lemon-verbena are placed to the back of the window, and lower-growing herbs such as parsley, oregano, and thyme grow up front. A calomondin orange gives fragrance to the air and tart fruits for marmalade. Hanging baskets of rose-geranium offer their leaves to jellies, teas, and cakes.

High above the teeming streets of New York City, man and plants keep each other company. Foreground plant is a *Dracaena Massangeana*. A *Philodendron Selloum* perches on the piano like a boom-town dance-hall girl and seems to be reaching out to join in a piece for two hands and leaf. More *D. Massangeana*, a fiddle-leaf fig, some orchids, a split-leaf philodendron, and a palm or two form the chorus.

Plants congregate like old friends in the sunny window of
architect Ray Listen's house. Many more plants could have fit
into the available space, but would adding plants improve on
the serene feeling that is here now?

Family room: Greenhouse onto a family room.
New rare orchids, lush tropical foliage, an
imposing but friendly lizard, goldfish, and pool
sharks live happily side by side. The greenhouse
measures 18 feet by 31 feet and is of the
free-standing type. Cost (the owner erected it
himself) ran around $7,000, including
foundation, plants, greenhouse, and fish.

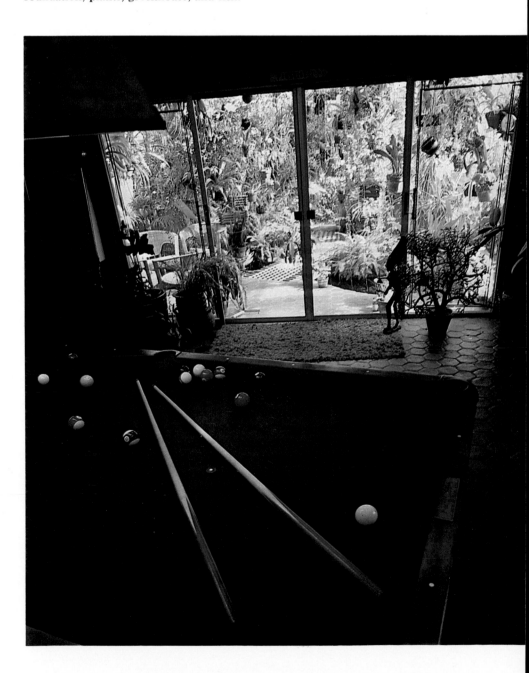

Here is a man who likes orchids and doesn't care who knows it. Believe it or not, this room is part of his New York City apartment.

These vary in size from those just a little larger than a standard bay window to the walk-in variety. The latter requires a foundation, of course, and can cost as much as a small wing. Greenhouses are discussed in detail in Chapter 6, The Family Room.

### Flavor and Fragrance

Chives, garlic-chives, and Egyptian onion are all members of the allium family and, besides tasting good, will protect you from sunstroke, garden moles, and vampires.

Most herbs can be started from seeds. Or, if you've been growing them outdoors, most of them can be transplanted into pots at the first sign of cold weather and brought inside. Well-developed herb plants are also sold at plant stores, and between the seed packets and the garden center you should be able to find what you want.

Some useful and flavorful herbs are basil, burnet, pot marigold, dill, fennel, marjoram, nasturtium, oregano, parsley, rosemary, sage, savory, sorrel, tarragon, and thyme. You can use their fresh leaves in cooking and you can also dry the leaves and store them near the stove in attractive bottles. Marjoram leaves are used as a seasoning, or for a garnish, and taste good when mixed with spinach. Rosemary is good in soup. Pot-marigold flowers can be used in place of saffron. Many herbs make good teas. Try sweet-marjoram leaves with a little mint; sage; balm leaves

Set out pots of herbs on a lazy Susan along with the salt and pepper and condiments. Keep individual scissors handy for snipping.

and a little lemon juice; rosemary and lavender. Use the leaves as you would ordinary tea leaves. Your herb tea will be green and pale but color isn't any indication of strength. Experiment with different herb combinations and package your own private blend for unique and personal gifts.

You can grow your herbs separately in pots on the sunny windowsill, but it's much more attractive to grow them together in trays or in hanging baskets. For a hanging basket, plant rosemary in the center for height, and surround it with thyme, sweet marjoram, parsley, and oregano. You can mix and match to your heart's content with herbs, and one or two of these airborne farms will supply the most voracious herb sprinklers with plenty of raw material. Just be sure to keep up with the watering requirements of your baskets, because they dry out more quickly than potted plants or tray gardens. Rosemary, for instance, is a goner if its roots are allowed to dry out the least little bit. Also remember to rotate the basket regularly so that light is allowed to reach all of the plants uniformly. Rotation also avoids the danger of the browning of leaves because of extended contact with the wall or the window glass.

Most of your herbs are going to be annuals and are going to be doing their best to produce flowers and go to seed. You've got to thwart them by pinching off the flowers and thus preventing the seeds from forming. This tricks the plant into thinking that it must keep on growing robustly in order to produce seed and thus reproduce itself. Some flowers are good to eat, though, so keep some nasturtiums and some pot marigolds blooming for salads and canapés.

For fragrance, you've got to have at least a couple of the scented geraniums. Keep them company with jasmine, sweet-olive, heliotrope, lavender, lemon verbena, and woodruff. Include some apple, orange, and pineapple mint.

The scented geraniums offer such a variety of fragrances that you might be tempted to use up all of your window space for their culture alone. You can grow geraniums that smell like roses, apples, lemons, nutmeg, and peppermint. These are not the heavily flowering garden types. The flowers of the scented geraniums are small and intermittent. But when you pick the leaves and crush them you are rewarded with delicious, spicy fragrance. The leaves add flavor to foods, too, particularly jellies, which can use apples for a base and to which are added the leaves of the rose-geranium. You can make tea from the leaves and they can also be used to flavor biscuits and cakes. Keep your geraniums on the dry side and do not overfertilize. Pinch back new growth from the top so that the sides will grow out into a heavy, well-formed plant.

### Pests

Inspect all of your plants at least once a month for insect pests such as aphids, whitefly, and red spider mites. If you find insect pests and must spray, for heaven's sake take your plants out of the kitchen, and preferably out of the house, before you spray. As a matter of fact, the use of deadly poisons to knock off a few tiny bugs doesn't make any sense at all. Many insects can be controlled with good old soap and water. If you've got aphids and/or scale, for instance, dip the entire plant in a tub filled with a weak solution of soap and water, or syringe the leaves thoroughly. This method will be particularly effective if a little nicotine is added. You smokers can make your own nicotine insecticide by soaking cigarette, cigar, or pipe tobacco in water for about a week. The drinkers in the family can do their bit, too, by donating some whiskey to your antibug program. A cotton swab soaked in Scotch, bourbon, vodka, or rum will put the most hardened mealybug under the table—for keeps. Of course, any alcohol will do. Just be careful to apply it to the bug and not the leaves; alcohol can burn the tissues. You can dislodge red spider, mealybugs, and aphids by taking the plants into the shower with you and forcefully spraying water on the leaves, particularly the undersides. If you

have a spray attachment on your water faucet, you can use that in the same way.

That extra time and trouble your homemade bug-control program takes is well worth it in order to avoid the use of persistent chemical insecticides. However, if your insect pests increase beyond your capability to keep them in line, you can use some of the relatively safe leguminous sprays. These sprays contain rotenone or pyrethrum, usually in emulsion with vegetable or mineral oils. They will normally control aphids, mealybugs, scale, whitefly, red spider, exposed thrips, and more. Look for them at your garden center and if you can't find them, ask to have them ordered.

Wash your plants thoroughly before using them in cooking, even if you've been using only plain soap and water for bug control.

### Kitchen Gardening

Starting plants from seed in the sunny kitchen window will yield you a surprising variety of garden vegetables. You'll be growing them for decoration and not abundance of crops, so don't plan on saving much money from your grocery budget.

You can grow radishes in pots as well as peas, parsley, pepper plants, leafy lettuce, and others. There is a tomato plant called 'Tom Thumb' which you should try. You can train the vine up and around your window and you can also expect to harvest a considerable number of delicious, tiny tomatoes. Plant the seeds according to directions on the seed packet. Keep the planted seeds in a dark place until they germinate, and then bring them into subdued light when the first sets of leaves appear. Finally place them in the sunny window after strong growth has been established and several sets of leaves have formed.

Another source of fruit and vegetable plants, and a very satisfying one since you're beating the system, is seeds and cuttings taken from the fruits and vegetables which you buy at the market. You've probably grown avocado plants from the large seed found in the fruit or have seen the beautiful tree that springs from the big, egg-shaped seed in friends' houses.

There are two ways you can grow yours: Fill a flowerpot three-quarters full of good potting soil and the last quarter with clean sand. Dig a hole and place the seed in it, broad end in the soil, so that about one-third remains above the sand. Keep the sand damp but not wet. You can also root the seed in plain water. Push toothpicks into the side of the seed, around it in a circle, and suspend the seed inside a glass (the toothpicks rest on the lip of the glass and support the seed). Fill the glass so that the bottom of the seed just touches the water. Put your seeds in a dark place, making sure that the sand is kept moist or that the water level is kept up to the seed in the glass. After six or seven weeks, a long white taproot will have developed and you'll know that it's time to move the seeds into the light. Soon a pale-green shoot will appear. The leaves will be small at first, but after you pot the seedling, strong robust growth will follow. After three sets of leaves have formed, pinch off the new growth. This will encourage branching and give you a more interesting-looking plant.

You can grow a pineapple plant from the one you buy in the store, but the method is different from that of the avocado. With a sharp knife cut off the rosette of leaves from the top of the fruit. Make your cut at exactly the place where this crown begins its growth from the body of the pineapple. Let the cut-off top dry out in the air for a day, a process which reduces the chances of decay, and press the top firmly into a flowerpot filled with clean mason's sand.

At first, keep your pineapple plant in a dim place and away from drafts. It should root in about five to eight weeks if you are careful never to let the sand dry out. When the crown is well rooted, transplant it to good potting soil and place in bright light. You'll know that it is doing well because it will develop a

Avocado   Date   Ginger

Acorn

Potato   Pineapple

Citrus seeds

Kitchen propagation.
Avocado: Place broad end in water and keep water level constant.
Date: Cover with sandy potting soil. Wait for palm tree to happen.
Ginger: Suspend in water by toothpicks until sprouted. Plant. Beautiful, rich, green foliage.
Acorn: You know what great things spring from little acorns. Be patient.
Sweet potato: Suspend in water with toothpicks. When eye sprouts and roots form, cut away and plant.
Pineapple: Dry out cut crown for a day and plant in sandy potting soil.
Citrus seeds: Dry off lemon, orange, tangerine, and grapefruit seeds. Put in a tray and cover with potting soil. Keep in a dark place until they sprout.

reddish sheen on its pointed leaves. Your pineapple plant is a bromeliad, and if you keep its crown filled with water, as you do all bromeliads, it will grow into a handsome houseplant. To induce flowering, dissolve five grains of calcium carbide in one quart of water. Fill the center of the crown with this solution and let stand for twenty-four hours, draining off the excess at the end of this period. In about five to six weeks you should be rewarded with the growth of a tiny new pineapple growing on the end of a stem emerging from the center of the crown.

Potatoes, sweet potatoes, yams, squash, and onions will root in plain water and can then be potted in soil. The sweet potato will grow into a lovely vine which can be trained around your window.

Look for ginger roots at your grocery store or in Chinatown. You can suspend them in water, as you did the avocado, and they will sprout. Follow the proceedure for avocados and bring into the light and plant in potting soil when good root development has occured. The foliage of the ginger plant is magnificent—a shiny dark-green.

After you have eaten your store-bought fruits, plant the seeds and grow your own trees. Even though they're just for decoration, your new plants will make you feel that you are finally getting your money's worth from the store.

The seeds from citrus fruits such as grapefruit, lemon, tangerine, and orange should be dried off and then planted in a sandy soil mixture, in a pot or tray. Plant a lot of seeds since some of them will not germinate. The seeds should be covered with a layer of soil equal in depth to the thickness of the seeds. Keep them in a dim, draft-free, warm spot until they sprout and then bring them gradually into the light. When they become sturdy little plants, transplant them to individual pots.

Try to grow apple, pear, peach, and plum plants, too. Surprisingly, you should have good luck in getting a date seed to sprout. These are large seeds so plant them, one to a pot, in four-inch pots.

Plant fresh peas, beans, and lentils, too. Your success in getting them to germinate will depend on what stage of development the plants were in when the crop was picked. If your peas are nice and tender, it means that they are immature and probably won't sprout.

The nuts that you buy in the store have probably all been roasted, a process which destroys the germ. You can ask at your organic-food store whether they have any unroasted nuts, and if you're lucky you can get these nuts to sprout. For surefire success, though, gather some

acorns from under an oak tree, and some winged maple seeds. These are sure to sprout, and if you've got a city apartment, an oak tree is a nice thing to have growing for you.

### Nooks and Crannies

Don't scoff at the idea that you have extra space in your kitchen for plants. You might have to get tough and throw out some pots and pans, the ones with the broken handles that you never get around to fixing, even that vacuum cleaner that hasn't worked in five years; but the result will be space that you didn't know you had. Probably enough for a small greenhouseful of plants.

Let's start on a tour of your kitchen, starting at the ceiling, and see where some plants could fit in. If your refrigerator isn't built in, is there space above for some hanging plants? You could build a waterproof box to fit on top of the refrigerator, too, and fill it with trailing *Philodendron oxycardium*, plectranthus, or some of the herbs. Plants like these do a wonderful job of softening the angular appliance look of your refrigerator. If you have cabinets over it, but there is at least one foot of space between cabinet and appliance, you can install fluorescent tubes and grow trays of low-growing herbs or even saintpaulias.

Do your kitchen cabinets extend right up to the ceiling or do they stop short, as many do, leaving a foot or so of space between cabinet and ceiling? If you have this extra room, fluorescent tubes will allow you to grow a bounty of edible and flowering plants. Select plants that are low-growing (you can keep herbs in bounds by frequent snipping), and avoid the ones that trail . . . you'll be constantly getting them caught in your cabinet doors. You can use part of your space up there for a vacation home for tired plants that have been seeing duty in the rest of the house. The warmth and excellent light will do wonders for them. Also, plants growing under lights can be brought down and used in ordinarily dark locations for special occasions. After a day

Fluorescent tubing allows you to grow plants in out-of-the-way places. These shelves were designed especially for plants, and tubing was incorporated under them and hidden by valances.

or two they should be returned to their original environment.

The section on light in Chapter 13 will give you all the information you'll need on the installation of fluorescent and incandescent lighting. Make sure that your fixtures operate from a switch separate from the one controlling the kitchen lights. This will allow you to control the amount of light your plants receive. An electric timer is a good idea, too, as it can be set to give your plants light for a few hours at night when you're asleep or over a weekend when you're away.

Plants in out-of-the-way spots will have to be removed periodically for watering and general inspection. Make this job easier by placing the pots on rigid metal or plastic trays. Don't use a tray that is too large; you'll grow to hate the chore of maneuvering a heavy load of plants down from a location above your head. Broiler foil, which is a fine water catcher for windowsills, is not a good idea for high places. You'll find yourself lifting the plants down pot by pot, an awkward and time-consuming job.

Is there room above your kitchen window to build a shelf for plants that trail down? Their hanging stems and leaves would receive good light from the window. *Philodendron oxycardium*, plectranthus, and the cissus vines would give just the right effect.

Can you spare the space and turn over one of your wall cabinets to plants?

Remove the door and the interior shelving. Build in a waterproof tray six inches deep, which should be deep enough to hold some pebbles and still hide the pots you'll be using. Now create a miniature landscape, keeping the larger plants to the rear and bringing the smaller plants forward. An interesting piece of driftwood or a rock can be added. Or, instead of a landscape, why not hang trailing baskets of ferns and other plants suitable for hanging? Or use the space to frame a single specimen plant such as a giant amaryllis, a huge clump of rosemary, a particularly well-formed podocarpus or polyscias? Even a Japanese bonsai would be appropriate. You can paint the interior (white is best if you need all the light you can get), or panel it with barn siding or other wood, or line it with mirrors for added dimension and light, or even paper it with large color blow-ups (such as the Sierra Club posters) of beautiful landscape photography. You'll probably need supplemental lighting; fluorescent-tube fixtures can easily be built into the cabinet.

Next we come to the space between the cabinets and the countertops. This is your precious work area and can hardly be classified as "out of the way." Perhaps you can do a bit of organizing and find room for a plant or two. A small bookcase could hold some plants, as well as their fluorescent lights, and your cookbooks, files, and telephone. Fluorescent lights placed up under the cabinets are good for your eyes, as well as for plant needs. How about designing and building an herb farm on wheels? The tray can be located under the lights most of the time, and when you have a large project and need the space, it can be rolled out of the way. This mobile landscape could be the focal point of your whole kitchen, particularly if space limitations dictate room for only one such planting. If you're going to grow herbs, introduce stones or pieces of driftwood. This will allow you to plant on different levels and you can select herbs for their upright or trailing qualities. If the unit is not too heavy, you can lift it onto the kitchen, or even the din-

ing-room table as a centerpiece for special occasions. Your family will soon find out how delightful freshly snipped herbs can taste, and as each person concocts his own special herb-seasoning formula, every meal can become a special occasion. Include space on the herb-farm tray for salt, pepper, mustard, ketchup, chutney, relish, and other favorite condiments. If enough light is available, you might decide to keep the whole unit on the table permanently. If you need extra light to do this, install a bright incandescent light directly over the herb garden, but high enough so that it will not burn the leaves. With an attractive shade of your choice, the light will furnish illumination for plants and people alike.

Continuing our tour of likely and unlikely locations for plants, we come to the under-the-counter cabinets and the various drawers found under countertops.

A fluorescent fixture installed under a countertop turns a drawer into a pull-out herb garden. You'll have to remove the back of the drawer so that there will be no interference with the light fixture when you pull the drawer out. Brace the sides with angle irons to make up for the loss of the support that the back furnished to the drawer.

The same fluorescent-light installation applies to the cabinets below. The lights enable you to grow plants up to three feet tall in there, or you can remove the door and build a miniature landscape like the one described earlier for wall cabinets.

Do you have a broom closet in your kitchen? With some rearranging of clean-

**Grow-lites illuminate herb garden in a drawer. Drawer pulls out for watering and harvesting.**

**The broom closet becomes an attractive addition to the kitchen decorating scheme and is a practical work space, garden center, and library.**

ing implements (you don't use all of those mops and squeegees anyway), and the removal of the door, you can have yourself a fantastic floor-to-ceiling garden. Again, the installation of fluorescent-tube lighting will allow you to plan this interior space to include plants on many levels. Build shelves to hold your recipe files, cookbooks, datebooks, and so on.

### The Eating Area

Up to this point we've been talking about plants that in some way lend themselves to the preparation of food, whether through their edible qualities or because they are visually appealing and resemble leafy garden vegetables in some way. Now let's look at plants that are good companions at the table, plants which impart a feeling of goodwill and *bon appétit*. Flowering plants are cheerful-looking and attractive on the table. Avoid violent colors and bizarrely shaped flowers, though. Blues, violets, and purples are not supposed good for the appetite, as most food manufacturers have found out through consumer research. Look for soft pastel pinks and whites in flowering plants. Creamy yellows and reds are good too. In foliage, stay away from thick, glossy,

vivid green and seek out the lime-greens and the soft greens variegated with white, light green, cream, or yellow. And stay away from prickly leaves, thorny stems, and tortuous shapes.

Some friends of mine kept these ground rules in mind while rebuilding their New York City brownstone, formerly a run-down rooming house. They designed a kitchen that took advantage of the generous ceiling height to indulge their love for green growing things. The eating area, which does double duty as a crafts and work area during nonmeal times, is framed with shelving made from construction lumber, 2 x 4s and 2 x 6s which were left unstained but which were sanded and waxed until they glowed. Fluorescent lights were installed under the shelves and furnish all the light for plants and people alike in this otherwise dark room. Lacy ferns and soft-pastel saint-paulias thrive. Behind the counter, hanging baskets of *Asparagus Sprengeri*, cissus, tradescantia, and hoya filter the light from the windows and furnish the only screening from the outside world. At the opposite end of the kitchen, where it joins the entrance hall and living room, the same kind of structure of waxed lumber, lights, and plants furnishes an effective, living screen which separates the kitchen from the rest of the house without diminishing the feeling of openness and space that is so important to maintain in city dwellings. This is the kitchen shown in color opposite page 57.

Years ago, I remodeled an old farmhouse. The original kitchen was long and narrow without an inch of extra space for decorating with plants. Of the two original windows, the one on the long wall was removed and the space was turned over to the range, oven, and charcoal pit. The remaining window was located on the narrow wall and was small and mean. We tore it out, enlarged the hole, and installed a beautiful bay window. Luckily the sink was located right in front of the window, and we loaded the space with plants, knowing that they would thrive in the humid atmosphere. This window planting is all the more effective because it is the only group of plants in the room and no one can fail to see it.

Transform your kitchen table or eating area into a garden gazebo by hanging baskets of ferns or other plants from the ceiling over the table. A combination hanging-plant and light-system can be devised so that the plants act as a shade for the light which illuminates the table below. You can incorporate hanging pots and utensils into this system, too. Special tools such as tongs, graters, long forks, shish-kebab skewers, herb scissors, and what-have-you all hang within easy reach. Softening the utilitarian look can be all sorts of plants that like to hang but that also taste good or smell delicious, such as spicy geraniums, lemon verbena, jasmine, parsley, savory, and rosemary.

If your table is near a wall, turn the wall itself into a display area for your elegant copper pots, tin molds, woks, wooden spoons, whisks, and other devices. Hang the pots and caldrons upright so that you can load them with pots of herbs and geraniums when they are not in use.

A glass-top table can be altered to include a shelf under the glass upon which you can place potted plants. (Years ago, glass and wrought-iron tables were sold with racks for plants.) This striking planting has some of the advantages of a terrarium, since moisture collects on the underside of the glass and adds to the relative humidity of the atmosphere around the plants.

**Create your own wall design using unusual implements, kitchen-oriented or not, which can serve as containers part of the time, or permanently, for potted plants.**

*Dracaena Massangeana*

# 6. The Family Room

Actually, any room in which the family gathers for relaxation is the "family room." But generally the term has come to mean a room, often in newer houses, additional to the dining and living rooms, where the more informal aspects of family life take place. "Recreation room" is another name (sometimes shortened to rec room). One builder I know even went so far as to advertise his houses as having "Hollywood Rumpus Rooms." Call it what you will, this particular room is subject to heavy traffic and plenty of action. Select plants for this environment that are as informal as the people who relax here.

Nearly all of the philodendron and ficus varieties are tolerant of drafts and temperature changes caused by constant opening and closing of doors and accidental knocks and bumps. The dracaenas are good and sturdy, too. If you've got active kids and animals, avoid the gracefully arching palms such as kentia. Bamboo, areca, and *Neanthe bella* palms have upright growth habits which make them more adaptable to heavily trafficked areas. Bromeliads are tough and forgiving. Group them in their pots or design and build a bromeliad tree for an out-of-the-way corner.

Make your larger plants mobile by attaching casters to their pots (see Chapter 3, The Living Room). This will enable you to move plants around according to need. A teen-ager's party, for instance, requires maximum floor space and the plants can easily be moved to the sides of the room to make way for dancing. An adult card party, on the other hand, can become a series of intimate groupings by separating the tables with the plants. After the games are finished, tables are folded and the plants can retreat to make way for refreshments. On weekends, when kids and grown-ups compete for space, trundle out the mobile plants and define private areas where each age group can do what it wants without bothering the others. Obnoxious kids' TV programs can be thus isolated from tender adult sensibilities and vice versa. Movable plants also make great screening devices for kids' toys, particularly when you're expecting company any minute and only have time to shovel the blocks, dolls, trains, and other apparatus into a corner. All you have to do is roll out the plants and station them between guest and mess.

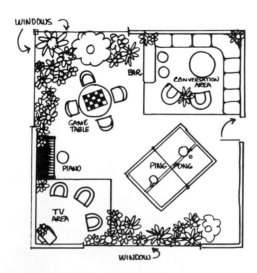

A. During the day, when the kids are in school, plants soak up the sun at the windows.

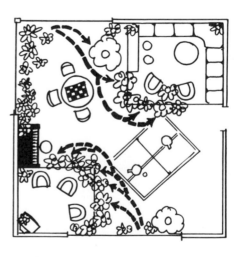

B. In the evening, when everybody's home, isolate special-interest groups (readers, students, TV viewers, chatters, etc.) by trundling plants into position where they can screen off various areas.

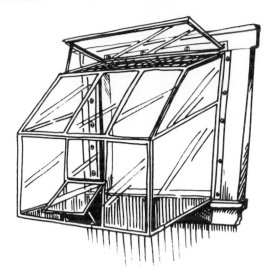

Hinged tops for ventilation and a bug screen are musts for any greenhouse. This window-sized one is easily installed. Attach to outside of frame for 50% more room. Remove entire window for easiest access.

A large bay window or dormer acts like a greenhouse if it faces south or southwest. East, southwest, west, and north exposures will also support plants, but northern illumination is sufficient only for foliage plants having a tolerance for low light levels.

## Greenhouses, from Tiny on Up

Greenhouses come in enough sizes and prices so that almost anyone can at least give some serious thought to installing one. Of course greenhouses are appropriate additions to any room, but the family room is especially suited because so much goes on there.

Window-type greenhouses, also called "reach-in" greenhouses, average around 150 dollars for a size which fits a window measuring 38 inches wide by 56 inches high. They are usually made of glass and aluminum and come ready for assembling (one manufacturer claims that this can be done by an unhandy man or woman in just a few minutes). Features to look for in a greenhouse of this type are a hinged top for ventilation and a bug screen. These greenhouses can be screwed right to your window frame or they can be attached to the house, outside of the frame. This latter method gives you about 50 percent more growing space for just a few dollars more. The best possible way to install a greenhouse like this is to remove the window frame completely so that your plants are always accessible from inside the room.

South or southeast is the best exposure, because of the morning sun. East, southwest, west, and north follow in that order. A north exposure will not give you the opportunity to be successful with flowering plants, but you should have good luck with many of the ferns, philodendrons, palms, ivy, and many more low-light-tolerant foliage plants. Supplemental lighting can be added to increase bloom where natural sunlight is spotty or of short duration.

In moderate climates, heat from the house is sufficient to warm these greenhouses. In locations where nights get really cold, a small electric heater can be installed to keep your plants at a comfortable temperature.

The more sun your greenhouse receives, the more you'll have to pay attention to your watering chores. Remember the sun sucks moisture from plants, soil, and surrounding air at a rapid clip. Keep

City greenhouses get plenty of sun and protect the plants from soot and other fallout. A person with one of these on his roof or terrace can face urban living with unusual serenity. Lean-to type is suitable for city or country. Shades are a must for hot summer days.

a pebble-filled tray at the bottom of your greenhouse and keep it brimming with water.

Next in size is the lean-to greenhouse. These also come in prefabricated form and are reputed to be installable in a day. If possible, locate the greenhouse over a door or window or an outside cellar door to make it accessible from the house. If none of these alternatives are possible, consider cutting a door or larger opening in the side of the house. If the side wall of your house is low, the floor of the lean-to greenhouse can be excavated and a retaining wall installed. For high side-walls with high windows, raise the greenhouse by building a retaining wall and backfilling in order to raise the entire greenhouse up to the required level. Always take advantage of building

Locate lean-to structures over door or window for accessibility from inside the house. Footing is necessary for this type, so figure it into the cost.

Even-span greenhouses can be erected free-standing or can be attached to the house at one end. This type can cost as much as new wing on the house.

irregularities such as corners and setbacks. They're often good places for lean-to greenhouses.

"Even span" greenhouses can be either free-standing or attached at one end to the house. The advantage of this type is more space and the opportunity to add onto the unattached gable end—as your enthusiasm and bank account increase.

Greenhouses of any size are great educational devices for the kids and lots of fun projects can be carried on in them. Starting seeds and tubers for the spring outdoor garden; taking leaf and stem cuttings (geranium cuttings started in November–December will be ready to bloom in the outdoor garden in April); propagating by layering, division, and offsets and runners are good indoor occupations for miserable wintery days. Refer to the section on propagation in Chapter 13, Plant Care, for complete directions for such projects.

Grow vegetables in your greenhouse during the winter months and lower the cost of living while raising the level of appetites. There's a new hybrid tomato called 'Pixie' which grows fourteen to eighteen inches tall and presents you with a heavy crop of bright delicious fruits the size of billiard balls. You'll be making fantastic bacon, lettuce, and tomato sandwiches about fifty days after the plants are set out.

Horticulturist Roger Wohrle's Upper Saddle River, New Jersey, greenhouse-den-showroom-laboratory-swimming-hole is a favorite year-round visiting place.

85

'Challenger' and 'Crusader' are hybrid cucumbers that are perfect for the greenhouse, even if it's only window size. Train the vines on strings or wires so that they arch across the roof bars of the greenhouse. Outdoors, insects carry cucumber pollen from blossom to blossom, but indoors you are going to have to handle the midwife chores yourself. Gather pollen on a soft camel's-hair brush and transfer it to another blossom. If you don't get around to this, your cukes will fail to develop.

For quick action to impress impatient youngsters, radishes can't be beat. Try 'Cherry Belle' and 'Icicle' for crisp and tender eating.

To round out your salad, try growing Bibb lettuce. 'Buttercrunch' is a good lettuce, too, with sweet and crunchy dark-green leaves. Do not cover your lettuce seeds with more than a quarter of an inch of soil, or they won't germinate. Head lettuce requires more room to grow in than you're likely to have, but you can start head-lettuce seeds in your greenhouse to use for setting outside in the spring.

Start watermelon and muskmelon seeds, too, to get a head start on spring planting. They'll produce much faster than plants started from seed planted outdoors. In climates where frost is a danger, wait until Mother's Day before you set out any tender plants.

The thought of growing herbs appeals to everyone's pioneer spirit. Somehow the thought of all-encompassing technology is less hideous if you've got a pot of rosemary or thyme growing for you. Grow herbs and scented geraniums in your greenhouse and feel good about life again. Chapter 5, The Kitchen, tells you how.

hibiscus

# 7. The Bedroom

Your bedroom should be an oasis of serenity, a room of peace. Since you spend one half of your life in this room, it's not only a good idea to decorate it with your own best interests in mind, it is mandatory. And the best way I know of to create a room environment that is calmly beautiful and good for the soul is to decorate with plants.

There are many plants that are particularly appropriate for use in the bedroom, but the other side of the coin is that there are some that are not such

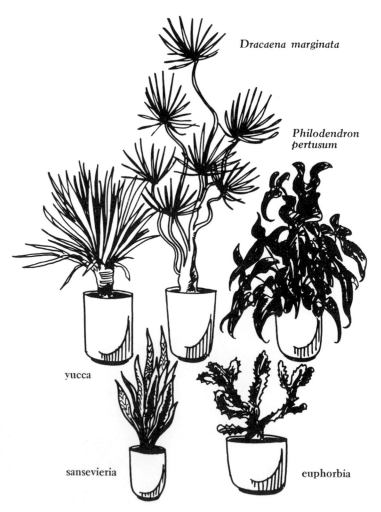

*Dracaena marginata*

*Philodendron pertusum*

yucca

sansevieria

euphorbia

**Avoid spiny, leathery, or tortuous-looking plants for the bedroom.**

good candidates. These are the plants which we'll discuss first.

*Dracaena marginata* could be criticized as being too contorted and tortuous of form if it were used in a setting that is supposed to be restful. The leaves of *Ficus decora* are too thick and leathery. *F. lyrata* is not so objectionable because it grows more gracefully and its leaves, although large, are more free-form in shape and have more character. Yucca is too spiny. So are all of the cacti. The thought of bumping into one of them in the dark is enough to make you stay in bed . . . regardless of the motivation to get up. Sansevieria is too unfriendly-looking for nighttime companionship. It's not called snake-plant for nothing. The large philodendrons—*P. pertusum*, *P. Selloum*, and *P. panduriforme*—are too massive and leathery for the bedroom. Besides, their ominous shadows cast upon the walls remind me too much of the creatures from which I was constantly trying to escape in childhood dreams.

The form and character of the plants you are looking for, then, should have grace, a lacy, feathery texture, a restful color, and above all a friendly attitude toward sleeping people.

### Restful Plants

Among the tall plants, the palms have just the right feeling for use in the bedroom. *Chamaedorea erumpens* looks like graceful bamboo and its fronds are comparatively broad. *Chrysalidocarpus lutescens* and *Howea Forsteriana*, the popular areca and kentia palms, are most gentle-looking. Of the two, the areca is more feathery and informal. Kentia is more elegant and formally graceful. *Rhapis excelsa* is a more closely bound palm and will enhance an area too small to accommodate its more freely growing cousins. *Phoenix Roebelenii* is usually available in either bush form or tree form and its foliage is similar to the areca's. *Cycas revoluta* (not a true palm, but quite palmlike) is a borderline candidate for the bedroom. It is graceful-looking but its long leaf stalks, with their many narrow and rigid leaflets,

Porch bedroom: This effulgent bedroom was once the back porch of a New York brownstone. Natural light floods into the room and plants thrive. Shades regulate the light on bright days and can be drawn at night for privacy.

**Bathroom:** Plants, lots of space, and shower with wild and wonderful tiles designed by Alexander Calder make this a room to reckon with in a Connecticut house by architect James Slavin.

**Bedroom:** A carefully placed grouping of artfully selected plants. The broad, languid leaves of the *Dracaena Massangeana* act as a foil for the more finely textured foliage of the *Ficus nitida, beaucarnea,* Boston ferns, and ivy.

Porch: Cacti and other succulents, a staghorn-fern, Boston
ferns, a sage-palm, Rex begonias, fatsia, and a variety of
hanging succulents bathe in the bright moist air of this
Victorian bay window in Prospect Park, Brooklyn. Humidity
is kept up by repeated mistings and by setting pebble- and
water-filled trays on top of the radiators.

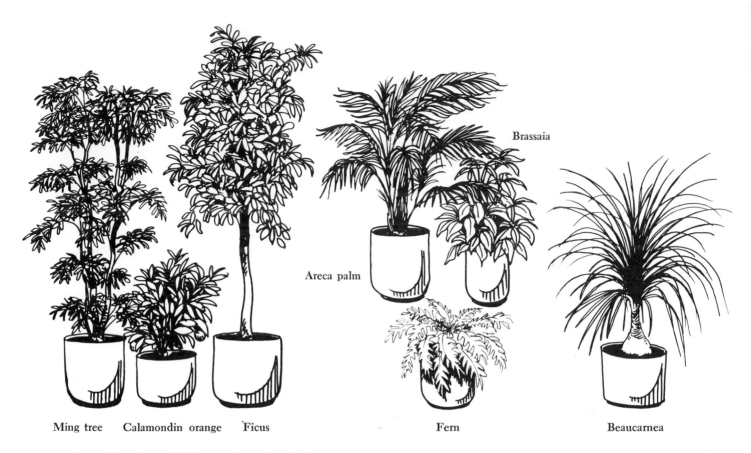

Ming tree    Calamondin orange    Ficus    Areca palm    Brassaia    Fern    Beaucarnea

**Graceful, calm, and relaxing plants for the bedroom.**

give it a somewhat stiff appearance when looked at closely.

Brassaia, often sold as schefflera, has leaves which are bright green and shaped like fingers. *Ficus nitida* and *F. benjamina* look like northern-climate, deciduous trees which have been pruned and tended by faithful, old-world grounds keepers. Their handsome lime-green leaves give these trees a refined and nontropical look. Also of value, if your decorating ideas lean away from the jungle look, are tree-form *Polyscias Balfouriana; Podocarpus macrophylla*, whose narrow, dark-green leaves resemble those of the yew; *Araucaria excelsa*, feathery, graceful, and ever-green-looking; and *Dizygotheca elegantissima*, which can be used as either nontropical- or tropical-looking, since its color is not lushly green but its form gives the impression of tall palm trees seen at a distance.

Medium-sized plants can be used to face down the tall plants, or can be used on tables or pedestals. *Cordyline terminalis* is a graceful plant that is usually available in heights of from one to six feet. Its relatives *Dracaena Sanderiana* and *D. Warneckii* will not grow so tall and they make a graceful multiple planting. Add spathiphyllum to your list for those areas in the room that receive low light. Keep it company with aglaonema and aspidistra. *Crassula argentea* is a medium-sized to small plant. It makes a striking specimen but needs good light. For a tropical-looking mass effect, try grouping pots of glossy-leaved, rich-green *Fatsia japonica*. They'll grow to about two feet tall.

Almost all of the ferns should be on your list of small plants for the bedroom. Their soft feather-pillow appearance and their ability to grow very well under medium light conditions makes them most useful. Use them in hanging baskets or as pedestal plants. Or let them spill over the edge of a table or chest of drawers.

There are many hanging plants that would be happy near a bright window in your bedroom. *Cissus rhombifolia* and *C. antarctica* are the well-known grape-ivy and kangaroo-vine. The latter has larger leaves which tend to hang more perpendicularly on longer stems. Tradescantia and *Hoya carnosa* hang in a similar fashion but their foliage is individually distinctive. *Tolmeia Menziesii* has soft-green, fuzzy leaves from which grow tiny new plants. Watch out for *Chlorophytum comosum*, though. It makes babies by lowering plantlets on multitudes of long, slender, thread-like stems. If you are uncomfortable at the thought of spiders, this plant would not be the best companion at naptime.

### Selecting Plants for the Way You Live

As you work out your decorating scheme and plant list, keep in mind how this room functions in the lives of its inhabitants. Do you get up in the morning, dress, and then leave the room until that night? Or is the room used during the day for reading, working, or occasional napping? Is a window kept open at night, regardless of the outside temperature, and then closed in the morning? This causes a drastic temperature variation from night to day and must be considered as a factor in selecting your plants. The quality of heat is important, too. Steam heat, for instance, is dry heat. Most plants like at least 50 percent atmospheric moisture, and while many plants can get by on less, ferns and saintpaulias like even more, from 50 percent on up to 70 percent and higher. Air conditioning dries out the air, too, so watch out for plants that cannot conform to your habits, beautiful as they may be.

Do you get some sun through the windows? How far does it penetrate the room, and what areas receive no direct sunlight, and what far corners get only low light levels?

It's a good idea at this point to begin to write all of this information down. Get a thermometer and record typical temperature readings taken periodically during the day and night, and over a representative period of a week or more. Make calculated guesses about seasonal differences in temperature. Get accurate light readings on all of the potential plant locations; the section on light in Chapter 13 will tell you how. Then carefully examine your own way of using the room. Perhaps it is used only for sleeping, so the door can be kept closed, and the heat kept down, during the day.

With your list of environmental conditions and uses of the bedroom in hand, you are ready to select plants which will thrive under these conditions. To take a shortcut at this point, or to promise yourself that you will alter the temperature and humidity situation to suit your plants, is to invite failure. As a case in point, *Ficus nitida*, a most decorative and desirable plant, cannot tolerate drastic changes in temperature. It's been known to partially or completely defoliate while being moved from the greenhouse to new locations in homes or offices. After being moved, the trees usually make a comeback, regaining foliage and in time adapting to the conditions of their new environment. But temperature that drops drastically at night and then soars during the day would cause even the most obliging *Ficus nitida* to drop its leaves permanently. Luckily, most ornamental plants will adapt themselves to the same conditions that we humans feel most comfortable in. The difference is, of course, that we can go out into the sun for light, or into the kitchen for a drink or a snack, or we can throw on a sweater if we are chilly, or take one off if we are too hot.

Now that we've made such a big thing about light and temperature, and so on, forget everything for the moment and make a list of all of the plants that you would like to have regardless of size and expense. Just daydream your way through a well-stocked greenhouse and mentally pick out everything that appeals to you. While you are doing this you'll probably be subconsciously shoving around chests of drawers and sliding the bed over a bit to accommodate the mythical new arrivals. Help your mental field trip along with constant references to garden magazines, pictures of attractive decorating schemes which you've clipped for your files, plant catalogs, and to the pictures and descriptions of plants listed in Chapter 2, Plants at a Glance.

Think about favorite vacations and outdoor experiences from your childhood and try to project yourself back into the scene to get a feeling about the landscape and foliage. Think about striking plantings which you've seen in other people's houses or in the movies or on television. All this time you should be writing madly. Put down plants whose names you know but also jot down descriptions of the kinds of plants that give you a good feeling when you are around them. After you've filled a page or two with your horticultural stream of consciousness, set about identifying each plant you've come up with by leafing through the color pages of Chapter 2.

Now back to reality. Some of your plants will have to be eliminated as possibilities for your bedroom because your analysis of conditions there show that they would not survive. But after some careful lining up of the plants that you like with the conditions that *they* like, you should end up with more than enough plants for a decorating scheme.

### Plants for Bedroom Windows

Windows, of course, are again your major light sources for natural illumination. If you are lucky enough to have at least three or four hours of sunlight during the day, flowering plants are a natural choice for that window. Try amaryllis and spring-flowering bulbs for forcing. Crotons, whose fantastically colored leaves give the effect of flowers, will flourish. So will kalanchoë, all of the over three hundred varieties of geraniums, lampranthus, Easter lilies, hanging baskets of *Hoya carnosa*, and trailing runners of hedera. You can frame your flowering window garden with sun-loving tall plants such as a matching pair of cypress or *Polyscias Balfouriana*, *P. fruticosa*, *Chamaerops humilis*, or brassaia. But watch out for brassaia (or schefflera, as it's often called). I've seen large specimens thriving in full sun and I've seen others that had been burned by

direct sunlight. My advice is to keep brassaia to the sides of a window, where it will receive good light but will not stand bathed in direct sun for hours on end. Rotate the plant (as you should all plants) so that it receives an equal amount of light on all of its leaf surfaces.

All of the citrus love direct sun, and if you can find a three-foot specimen calamondin orange, or two, they will serve nicely as an underplanting to the flowering plants in the window. *Pittosporum Tobira* and *Ligustrum lucidum* would do the job for you too, or small sizes of these plants could be placed in front of the citrus specimens.

*Beaucarnea recurvata* is a lovely, palmlike plant with long, arching leaves. It likes direct sun and might have a place in your sunny window. Gardenias like sun, particularly when in bud. Keep them budding with heavy feedings of a balanced plant food and also applications of ferrous sulphate.

Above all keep gardenias and other sun-loving plants well watered. Direct sunlight quickly evaporates water transpired through the leaves of the plants. Water vapor in the air is soon exhausted, too. Even though sun-loving plants are adapted to dry conditions, you will have to replace the water lost through evaporation in order to encourage their growth. Place easily refillable pans of water among the plants, or build permanent, waterproof trays that will hold all of the plants. Fill the trays with pebbles, so that the pots are kept above water level, and keep them full of water. In this way the humidity of the atmosphere around the plants is kept at the maximum and your watering chores are kept to the minimum. You probably won't have to fill the tray more than once a week.

### Group Plantings

Plants with similar environmental needs grow much better when grouped together. I won't go so far as to say that they enjoy each other's company and welcome the opportunity to talk things over (although

I sometimes wonder), but they can certainly benefit mutually from the increase in humidity in their surrounding air which results from the increased area of moist soil and transpiring leaf surface. Watering, feeding, and other maintenance tasks are made easier, too, when you group your plants together.

But the most important thing to you, the decorator, is that grouping plants together in interesting ways offers you the opportunity to work with other natural objects in your design. A miniature waterfall or a serene pool full of tropical fish are certainly appropriate elements in a grouping of tropical plants. You can even add cherished bits of memorabilia—a piece of driftwood collected on a winter's walk along the beach, shells, bits of colored glass softened and polished by the waves, smooth pebbles gathered from a mountain stream, pieces of sculpture, pottery objects, a favorite wood carving, unusual containers, a painting by Rousseau, or a favorite photograph framed by green, growing plants. As you add personal and beloved objects to your miniature plant world, you are offering something of yourself to the plants. In a sense you are joining with them to show a richer, fuller part of yourself. The association of people and plants is so natural for the home—after all, we've been living together now for at least two million years.

Unfortunately professional decorators who design interiors for office buildings and other commercial establishments fail to recognize the relationship that people and plants enjoy together. They place plants in sterile, "decorator" planters and spot them here and there in a forlorn effort to disguise a fire extinguisher or to soften a stark architectural detail. The plants look alien and cut off from the living. To me they look rather embarrassed to be there, and I've often felt like giving them their freedom, just as I would like to do for animals in the zoo. Your own imagination, good taste, and humanity will steer you clear of "bank lobby" planting. Just treat plants as friends and not things.

## Unusual Ways to Use Plants

If a dressing table is part of your bedroom furniture, try transforming it into a woodsy bower by framing the mirror with *Ficus nitida* or some tall palms. Place pots of *Philodendron oxycardium* at either side of the mirror and train the quick-growing runners to strings or wires framing the mirror. Turn one drawer over to plants and set in a waterproof tray and a trailing cissus vine.

Transform your bed into a fern grotto or a vine-covered treehouse. For the grotto, surround your bed with tall palms, leaving only the foot of the bed open for getting in and out. Build a row of glass tanks across the bed where the headboard would be on more conventional beds (fish aquariums do very well for the tanks). Plant the tanks with moisture-loving, woodsy ferns, such as the davallias and the adiantums, and hang a few more hardy nephrolepis varieties in baskets just above them. Since it will be rather dark in this hideaway, even during the day, add supplemental fluorescent or incandescent lighting which you can leave on during the day for the ferns, and also read by at night.

The treehouse effect comes about when you train *Philodendron oxycardium* to cover the headboard and to grow out over the bed on wires which you've attached to the ceiling. To add to the feeling of height, place medium-sized plants on the floor on either side of the headboard so that you look out over the tops of the plants when you are lying down, instead of looking up at them. If you are courageous and really want to feel that you are sleeping on top of the world, paint the ceiling sky-blue and add some white, fluffy clouds.

If you are decorating from scratch in your bedroom, why not coordinate the wallpaper, bed linen, and drapery colors and patterns with your plants? Either choose your surroundings to match your plants in some way, such as in color or form, or do it the other way around and pick the plants that echo your chosen color scheme. To really show off your

Use a bookcase for a headboard. Install fluorescent lighting for plants and reading. Add books, radio, TV, movie projector, bar, what-have-you. Enclose within a bower of tall palms and jump in for the best rest you've had in years.

plants paint everything white—walls, floor, furniture, and accessories. Find linens, bedspread, draperies, and rugs of the same shade of white. Your room will appear bigger and brighter. As a matter of fact, you'll be able to keep plants in corners that would have been too dark in your former color scheme.

Mirrors bring light into the room, too, as well as giving you more visual space. A wall of glass seems to double the size of the room and plants placed in front of it are reflected, giving the impression that the room extends beyond the wall. A trick which was explained in the chapter on the living room, and which I've also used successfully in outdoor garden designing, will heighten this optical illusion in a bedroom, too. Place the mirror at an angle to the wall so that it reflects the plants which have been placed in front of it, but never reflects you, the viewer. Arrange the furniture across the room from the mirror so that it is not reflected, and adjust the angle of the mirror to compensate for items which cannot be placed elsewhere. Disguise the edges of the mirror with tall plants and the illusion is complete. From your bed

you should have the impression that you are looking through an open doorway that leads into an endless garden. It's a nice thing to wake up to in the morning, and if you are a city dweller this mirror trick can bring the precious feeling of space into your often cramped environment.

Plants can be used as partitions and room dividers in a bedroom. Instant closets are formed by lining up a row of tall plants and hanging clothes behind them. Or use the plants to form a hidden sanctuary where sewing, knitting, reading, meditating, or dressing can be done in privacy. If you use your bedroom for living during the day, partition off the bed with plants and move them aside at bedtime.

If you've heard, as I did when I was little, that plants should not be kept in the same room where people sleep, this explanation should set your mind at ease on the subject: Years ago, nurses in many hospitals would remove all plants from the room at night, explaining that they used up too much oxygen. This is true to an extent about cut flowers, which are undergoing a process of slow wilting and decomposition. Growing plants are *adding* oxygen to the air during the day, however, and while they do reverse the process and absorb some oxygen at night, the amounts are negligible.

### The Children's Room

Your child's bedroom is a classroom on *his* terms. It's a place where he can privately review events and experiences and try to make some sense out of them. It's a secret sanctuary for his prized possessions, which give him comfort because they are familiar and unchanging. The sometimes strange and unlikely things which he picks up and brings home for his own private reasons teach him about the nature of things: texture, color, weight, form, thickness, and tensile strength; how they chip or melt or dissolve. They serve as memory joggers, too, and their presence helps to recall pleasant experiences.

Kids love plants and flowers and will welcome the responsibility of keeping them in their rooms, if a little time is taken to point out the similarity between plant and human needs. It's up to you to make the arrival of plants into your child's private world an exciting and important event, so that growing things can take their place among his other cherished treasures.

### The Nursery

As you've found out, you spend a lot of your time in the new baby's room, and flowering plants can help to cheer you both up, particularly at those weird night-time feeding hours.

Saintpaulias are as softly colorful as Baby's blanket, and their leaves are as fuzzy. Hyacinths, narcissus, and tulips can be grown, in season, and so can lilies and potted azaleas. Citrus plants, like calamondin orange, flower freely and fill the air with perfume (an advantage during diaper changings).

Temperature is an important consideration in selecting plants for the nursery. You'll be keeping the heat at a fairly constant level, so avoid trying to grow plants, such as camellia, that require a considerable drop in temperature at night.

For the sunny window, try some of the many varieties of geranium. A shelf or table full of them will supply you with a wealth of color which you can rotate throughout the room for bright and cheerful accents. Geraniums are easily found in nurseries and greenhouses during the outdoor growing season but are scarce in winter. You can anticipate the arrival of the geranium shortage and pot up those growing outdoors in your garden, or take cuttings from them (Chapter 14 tells you how). You can even keep geraniums over the winter by drying them out and hanging them in bunches in a cool, dry place. When you are ready to repot them, give them a good soaking and trim back the dried up, obviously dead leaves and stems.

Of course you will be careful to keep any plants out of the reach of the baby. Apart from the danger of his pulling a pot down upon himself, the leaves of certain plants could, if chewed or eaten, make him ill. You have probably heard that some plants are dangerously poisonous. This is true, but the list is small and such plants are not offered for sale. The following list of dangerous plants is included, however, as a reference in case you are ever in doubt about a plant or cut flower.

### Contact Poisons

Poison-ivy and poison-sumac. There are at least three poisonous species.

Cypripedium. The pink lady's-slipper is occasionally somewhat poisonous.

Primula. One greenhouse variety is very irritating to some people. It is *Primula obconica*.

Urtica. The nettles are more of a nuisance. The stinging sensation which they cause is usually not long-lasting.

### Internal Poisons

*Acontium Napellus*. Monkshood. All parts dangerous.

*Arum maculatum*. Lords-and-ladies. All parts dangerous.

*Atropa Belladonna*. Belladonna. All parts dangerous.

*Cicuta maculata*. Water-hemlock. All parts dangerous.

*Conium maculatum*. Poison-hemlock. All parts dangerous.

*Datura Stramonium*. Jimsonweed. All parts dangerous.

Delphinium. Most of the larkspurs. Foliage dangerous.

Digitalis. Foxglove. Foliage dangerous.

*Helleborus niger*. Christmas rose. Root a violent heart poison.

*Hyoscyamus niger*. Henbane. The juice is deadly.

Kalmia. Both the native laurels. The foliage is dangerous.

*Laburnum anagyroides*. Golden-chain. Seeds dangerous.

*Nerium Oleander*. Oleander. All parts very dangerous.

*Phytolacca americana*. Poke. Root dangerous.

*Prunus serotina*. Wild black-cherry. Wilted foliage very dangerous. Also the related *Prunus virginiana*.

Rhododendron. All species. Foliage dangerous.

*Ricinus communis*. Castor-oil plant. Seeds deadly.

*Solanum nigrum*. Deadly-nightshade. Wilted foliage deadly.

*Taxus baccata*. Yew. Leaves and fruits dangerous.

Amateur doctoring is folly because these are serious poisons. Some have a narcotic effect which might go unnoticed, because children naturally become drowsy during the day. At the least suspicion of poisoning by a plant (look for pain, headache, vomiting, drowsiness, convulsions), send for a doctor at once and show him a specimen of the plant suspected of causing the trouble.

Getting back to the friendly kinds of plants—your baby's room is a good place for foliage plants and there are some which are soft-looking and resemble familiar objects. Ferns are fluffy and teddy-bearlike. Most palms are feathery and airy-looking, and so are *Polyscias fruticosa* and *Dizygotheca elegantissima*. Stay away from the massive philodendrons and rubbery ficus varieties. A plant that looks nice

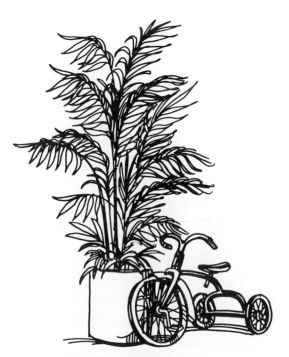

**Choose plants that are gentle and friendly-looking for little people's rooms.**

95

and friendly during the day can appear tall and threatening when seen through sleepy nighttime eyes.

### The Terrible Twos

As your toddler gains mastery over horizontal navigation he begins to notice that the world goes up, as well as backward, forward, and sideways. During this time nothing is safe no matter how high it is placed and how far out of reach it seems to be. Displaying the climbing skill of a Sherpa guide, he will find invisible toe and finger holds in his crib, chairs, dresser, even the walls. No fragile plants and brittle flowerpots are safe during this alpine period if they are placed on a high surface. Give him plants that are as big and strong as he is and set them firmly on the floor in tilt-proof pots.

Most of the philodendrons are as tolerant of abuse as a large family dog. They also don't look as if they might be very good to eat. Their leaves are broad and thick and their stems are strong. If some pieces do get broken off, they are quick to compensate with new growth. *Philodendron pertusum* and *P. panduriforme* are usually purchased already trained to grow on bark or a slab of wood.

**Kids should grow up with plants, but the plants should be stalwart enough to survive rough-and-tumble friendship.**

The wooden support furnishes an excellent anchor and even the most determined fingers will have trouble prying loose the tightly attached air roots of the plant. *Philodendron oxycardium* can be planted in these pots, and its trailing runners will hide the soil and discourage digging.

*Ficus elastica* and *F. pandurata* are good, sturdy plants with woody, break-resistant stems. Like the philodendrons, they like a warm temperature but do not require excessive moisture or humidity. They do require more light than the philodendrons, though, and should be located in the room with this consideration in mind. I particularly like *Ficus pandurata* for a child's room because its textured, rich-brown bark and bright-green leaves are very alive and organic-looking. The plant grows in interesting, free-form ways, too, which give it a personality of its own and invite the child to create imaginary associations with it.

Watch out for kids and palms. The long, graceful fronds are not tolerant of rough handling. One day my son Adam, a well-coordinated, brilliant two-year-old at the time, noticed that the two kittens had climbed onto the pot of a very tall and beautiful areca palm, and were digging a hole in the soil. Adam had been scolded for doing the same thing; and now he was in a position of authority, no kitten was going to get away with digging holes in the potting soil while he was around. The chase must have been magnificent! Later we decided that the kittens must have made it to the top of every one of the dozen or so graceful fronds. Adam, being a lot heavier, however, only made it halfway up before they bent and broke. All twelve! As a further note on personal experience, disasters such as this one were few. Children are quick to grasp the importance of gentle handling, particularly when they see the results of rough treatment. Once they learn that plants are alive and that they respond to watering, good light, gentleness, and love, your troubles, as far as breakage and improper treatment go, are just about over.

### Early School Years

Your child is learning at a rapid pace during these years, and he is eager to show you his school projects and tell you about his adventures. You can help him to keep the excitement of the learning experience going at home by letting him tend to the needs of strange and wonderful plants in his room.

Select active plants for children of this age. The wonders of seed germination will be lost on a little mind that seeks rapid-fire cause-and-effect relationships in his activities. Flowering bulbs are a good idea once growth pushes through the soil. Some plants catch flies and eat them, and the Venus's flytrap is reported to respond hungrily to raw hamburger meat. *Philodendron oxycardium* grows so fast you can almost see it reach out to climb higher on a string or wire support. *Citrus mitis* blossoms fragrantly and then produces exciting, real oranges which ripen from green to bright orange.

Saintpaulias have beautiful flowers and reproducing them by taking leaf cuttings is fun. Peperomias, gloxinia, many begonias, and such succulents as crassula, kalanchoë, sedum, and echeveria can be propagated by leaf cuttings, too. Ferns can be propagated from runners or rhizomes. Tip cuttings from scindapsus and other plants will take root and grow into new plants. The leaves of *Begonia Rex* can be cut into sections containing a piece of primary vein, and new plants will develop when the sections are placed in sand. Propagation projects like these are easy and fun. The baby plants can be potted and given to school friends and to members of the family as gifts.

Some plants make propagation so easy for you that all you have to do is to stand around with a pot of soil and a pair of scissors. These plants produce offsets, which are small plantlets. If they are allowed to strike soil, they will root easily after being snipped from the parent plant. Episcia, saxifraga, and Chlorophytum are examples. (See the section on propagation in Chapter 13.)

A sturdy table serves as a work area for plant projects. Reference books and tools are all within easy reach, and materials such as soil and fertilizer are kept in lidded canisters. Area doubles as desk and study hall for school subjects.

## Later School Years

Plant projects abound for the older child, and his room can be turned into a plant conservatory if he is so inclined. Grafting, air layering, and hybridization are exciting projects which the interested child can carry out right in his own room.

You should plan the room around these projects so that your budding naturalist will be able to work in an area set aside for plants and will not have to pack up shop to accommodate other activities. A sturdy table with a washable surface is a must. There should be a lip around the top so that the inevitable soil and water spills won't cause too much inconvenience. There should be a sunken recess, or well, in the tabletop in which soil can be mixed and stored. There should be a cover for this soil bin. There should be shelves for fertilizer, tools, empty containers, and books. Include a cupboard with doors so that germinating seeds, bulbs, and other darkness-requiring pro-jects have a place to be stored. There should be a rack for trowels, tampers, sieves, picks, clippers, scissors, wire, and other tools of the trade. Include a source for artificial illumination such as a ready-made fluorescent growing-light unit.

A youngster's room of even the most modest dimensions will often yield a surprising number of out-of-the-way corners in which a plant or two can be grown. A shelf in the closet can be easily outfitted with a fluorescent-tube fixture, and some brightly colored caladiums or saintpaulias can be grown there. Plant them in trays that can be easily removed for inspection and watering. A similar arrangement can be made to fit under the bed. In fact, this entire area can be rigged with fluorescent lighting and a magnificent garden can be trundled in and out. This under-the-bed conservatory can conceivably furnish the whole house with a constant supply of healthy, flowering plants.

Hi-fi components nestle behind Amazonian jungle; controls are reached by rustling around in the foliage. Seedlings sprout under bed, nurtured by fluorescent tubing.

## Adolescence

At this stage in life, your teen-aged sons or daughters aren't going to be overly interested in plant growth, since they've got their own to keep them occupied. Spare space may be scarce or nonexistent in their rooms, too. Plants are still important, though, and might even exert a bit of calming influence over the occupants.

The adolescent bedroom is a high-activity area and plants should be kept out of the line of fire of hurtling bodies, tossed clothing, and poorly aimed textbooks. Group plants together near a window or in any well-illuminated spot that isn't in the way. If you can, get your child involved with you in building a naturalistic setting for personal possessions such as that discussed earlier in this chapter for your own bedroom. Childhood treasures can be dug up and used in appealing ways, particularly in a girl's room. Prop a much-hugged doll against an interesting

rock and surround her with some other childhood mementos, saintpaulias, and ferns. Add a tumbling waterfall and a pool with fish to keep her company in her retirement. The same idea can be carried out in a more masculine way to display a worn-out baseball glove that was once the wonder of the Little League or the track shoes that beat Central in the four-forty back in your son's sophomore year.

Plants can be used to hide a hi-fi speaker system, or even the turntable, amplifier, and other components. Space behind a screen of plants provides a great catchall for laundry, books, athletic gear, and other paraphernalia. If you place the plant tubs on casters, the plants can be rolled about the room and placed as needed for screening purposes.

It's your daughter's room that will probably offer the most rewards for decorating efforts. The two of you can put your heads together and work out some strik-

**Limited bedroom space calls for a convertible sofa or studio couch. Plants bring elegance and coziness to space.**

ing schemes in which plants figure prominently, and perhaps even set the stage for some new furniture purchases. Palms suggest Victorian furniture: an oak headboard, chest of drawers, and rocking chair, all of which have been stripped of paint and varnish and have been taken down to the natural wood. Or they suggest a Mediterranean villa overlooking the cobalt sea: whitewashed walls with mossy niches filled with ferns; a heavy, chocolate-brown Spanish chest under the fronds of a bamboo-palm; a lime-green canopy of ferns over a wrought-iron bed. Palms are good companions to contemporary furniture, too. Their curving planes emphasize the sharp, architectural angles of a Parsons table. A pair of palms at either end of a simple studio couch transforms it into a jungle bower.

**Alcalphya giodseffiana**

# 8. The Bathroom

Since the advent of modern plumbing, 3,600 years ago on the island of Crete, few esthetic breakthroughs have been made in the design of sinks and tubs and toilets. Therefore, it's fairly safe to assume that any artistic improvements in your own porcelain palace will have to be carried out by you. Fortunately, there are a wealth of humidity-loving plants that are perfect for bathroom situations. Here is a partial list:

Aglaonema; *Asparagus plumosus, A. Sprengeri;* araucaria; caladium, cryptanthus; dieffenbachia; *Dracaena Godseffiana, D. terminalis, D. marginata, D. Massangeana;* euonymus; ferns—adiantum, asplenium, cibotium, davallia, nephrolepis, platycerium, polypodium, pteris; *Hoya bella, H. carnosa, H. motoskei;* palm; philodendron; pilea; *Begonia Rex;* saintpaulia; scindapsus; syngonium; *Tolmiea Menziesii;* tradescantia.

## High Humidity, Low Upkeep

The bathroom is usually the most humid room in the house. Aquatic activities such as showering, bathing, washing, rinsing, and flushing add a good amount of water vapor to the air. After living in your bathroom for a while, many of the plants in this chapter will think that they are back home in the rain forest. High humidity is important to the plants that we'll discuss, but they'll also need your attention as to light and temperature.

## Don't Turn Off the Lights

Bathrooms usually have plenty of artificial illumination, since one needs good light in order to do a good job of putting on makeup or taking off whiskers. Also, if my experience is typical, lights are left burning in bathrooms all over America by forgetful children and adults. Therefore, why not leave the bathroom lights on most of the time, on purpose, and allow a generous planting to be the beneficiary? Remember, though, that plants, like humans, need some rest. The last member of the family to bed should be charged with turning off the lights.

To make sure that your bathroom lighting furnishes a sufficient amount of illumination for good plant growth, you should thoroughly acquaint yourself with the section on light in Chapter 13. Keep in mind that your bathroom plants will normally receive about sixteen hours of illumination if you leave the lights on during waking hours. Therefore, your foot-candle reading need not be as high as that required by plants receiving light over a period of daylight hours only. If your existing lighting gives from 500 to 1,000 foot-candles over a sixteen-hour period, plants selected for their shade tolerance will thrive.

## Keep Nights Cool

During the period of darkness, try to keep the temperature down as much as possible. Lowering the temperature by as much as twenty degrees at night allows plants to carry manufactured sugars from their leaves to their stems and roots. Should this process be hindered, food manufacture will be curtailed and your plants will suffer. Choose plants that have similar temperature requirements (you'll find this information next to each plant listed in Chapter 2, Plants at a Glance). It's much easier to keep them happy that way.

## A Screen of Green

Unless your bathroom window looks out on an uninhabited expanse of tundra, you probably like to shade or curtain your bathroom window in some way, particularly at night. How about a screen of green, growing plants?

**Hanging pots of cissus make an effective window screen (unless your bathroom window looks out on somebody's living-room window).**

One easy way to place plants in the window is to build or attach brackets that will support glass shelves; glass allows light to pass through to plants on lower shelves. Plants should not touch the window in cold weather, so provide as much room as possible between plant and pane. You are lucky if your window faces east or west because that's where the best light is. South is ideal for winter, but watch out for prolonged direct sunlight on some plants.

Ferns make terrific window plants, provided that they're not subjected to drastic temperature drops (winter cold comes right through window glass).

Magnificent bird's-nest fern soars majestically near the roof of horticulturist Roger Wohrle's greenhouse.

Many ferns screen nicely without appearing massive, and light filtering through their fronds bathes the room in a soft green aura.

Explore the nephrolepis ferns which include N. *exaltata*, the familiar and well-loved Boston fern. This old friend has given us many interesting variations on its stiff-fronded, upright character, such as the more lacy *Whitmanii* and the densely fluffy *Wrightii*.

The most engaging of the polypodium ferns is *P. aureum*, the hare's-foot fern. It has a mat of furry brown rhizomes that will enchant the kids. *Mandaianum* is a wavy-leaved variation and *Knightiae* is suitable for shelf or hanging basket.

One of my favorite ferns is *Asplenium Nidus-Avis*, the bird's-nest fern. It's got long, unusually shaped, lemony-green leaves which are translucent and arranged in rosettes. It is a good recommendation for a window-screening plant.

There are other lovely ferns, such as pteris, davallia, cibotium, and adiantum, which have great possibilities for your bathroom decorating scheme, but which would not give you the screening effect you'll be looking for. We will take a look at them further on in this chapter in other contexts.

If you're feeling adventurous and are willing to take a chance on some touchy plants, try generous pots of billowing *Asparagus plumosus* or *A. Sprengeri*. I call

*Dracaena Massangeana* **canes carry foliage up high, a boon for small spaces.**

them touchy because I've never had much luck keeping them going for more than a couple of months. However, they are inexpensive, readily available, and give a fresh, yellow-green, ferny effect.

If you've got room in front of your window for some pots, you can place larger plants there, such as palms for an effective screen. *Dracaena Massangeana* canes of different heights will give you an interesting pattern of vertical "trunk" elements topped at various levels by sprays of long, arching leaves of rich green, longitudinally striped with light-green and yellow.

If your floor space is too limited, there's always the ceiling. From it you can hang a cloud of plant containers directly in front of the window. Hang them on a variety of horizontal and vertical planes for maximum screening effect and good air circulation. Your plant supplier will furnish you with plants already potted in containers suitable for hanging. I think that the open basket type is the most attractive, but you can convert any pot, plastic or terra-cotta, into a suitable hanging container, by attaching string, wire, etc. Among some beautiful flowering

trailers are the hoyas. *Hoya bella. H. motoskei* and *H. carnosa* put forth many stems bearing gray-green or green oval leaves. Fragrant pink flowers appear after the plants have become acclimatized (be patient, this might take a couple of years). You'll find lots more hanging-basket plants at your supplier's and *Tolmiea Menziesii*, the piggyback-plant, the pileas, and the various ivies will be among them. Avoid the temptation to bring home the lavish hanging-basket geraniums and fuchsias, even though they match your towels. The geraniums won't like the humidity of your bathroom, and many of the fuchsias offered are unsuitable for indoor growing.

Matching bathroom linens, both in color and texture, is an idea to be considered, however. There is a wealth of color and design available in the bath linen line these days. You should be able to find just the right shade of green or the perfect floral design to complement your plants.

## Make Horizontal Surfaces Work for You

Horizontal bathroom space is usually limited to the floor, to the sink or vanity top, and to the top of the toilet tank. If you can spare the floor space, a tall specimen plant can be the focal point of your bathroom. The dracaenas are good choices because they take up very little horizontal space. *Dracaena marginata* can be trained to exhibit all of its foliage at eye level or above. *D. Massangeana* canes can be used in the same way. The philodendron family also offers a choice of handsome plants that like to climb and therefore occupy a minimum of horizontal space. If your bathroom is exceptionally large, and floor space is not at a premium, *araucaria excelsis*, the Norfolk Island pine, would be great. Its graceful habit and soft green needles seem to me to be the essence of the temperate rain forest. Depending on your ceiling height and space requirements, you'll find many more candidates in Chapter 2, Plants at a Glance. Just remember to avoid plants that require dry

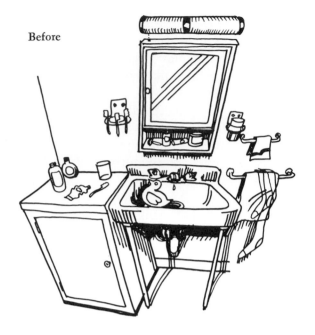

Before

After

**Keep plants off work area. Group them for best effect. Check for plants which tolerate low light and for some that grow in water only.**

conditions, like the schefflera and, of course, cacti and other succulents.

Sink tops and vanities are handy repositories for toothbrushes, toothpaste tubes, makeup, colognes, shaving gear, Kleenex, headache tablets, vitamins, and plastic ducks. Perhaps the calming effect of a serene grouping of plants can bring order to this chaos. There's no need to take up work space, though, if you keep

your plants to the sides or group them in an area of their own. You can even do away with soil-filled pots if you wish, because many plants will grow in just plain water. Try philodendron, aglaonema, syngonium, and tradescantia. Place them in attractive glasses, vases, jugs, or what-have-you, and add a bit of charcoal to each for sweetening.

A counter top is a great place for growing saintpaulias, or African violets, provided the light is sufficient. If it is not, you can build glass shelving closer to your light source. In many bathrooms the major source of illumination is around or above the mirror. By grouping shelves near this source and, if necessary, altering the arrangement of the lights, a number of design possibilities present themselves. What better way to start the day than to first glimpse your sleepy face surrounded by a halo of delicate pink and blue flowers?

Ferns are a good bet for the vanity top, too. A variation on the above idea is the same type of shelf, minus the fluorescent lights, with a line of ferns marching across the top. In this instance, toilet articles can be neatly stored beneath the shelf. The fresh, green *Asplenium Nidus-Avis* would be a good choice because of its upright habit. So would the

**Humans need all the help they can get in the morning. African violets provide a lot.**

Heroic staghorn-fern clings to a suspended slab of wood.

nephrolepis and polypodium ferns. For a light, airy look, try adiantum, or the maidenhair-ferns. Their stems disappear against a dark background and their leaves float in space like hundreds of green flying saucers. Be warned, however, that this fern is notoriously touchy about being moved from greenhouse to home. It would be a good idea to bring a single plant home as an advance guard and see

how it reacts. While you are at the greenhouse, ask to see the davallia ferns. You'll be surprised that such an amazing amount of delicate fronds and long, furry rhizomes could spring from such a relatively small pot of soil. Your greenhouse will also undoubtedly have several of the platycerium ferns on prominent display. These are the strange and exotic staghornferns which can be purchased usually

107

Exotic staghorn-ferns tolerate low light and can be an answer for problem areas.

attached to bark or wood and hung at home on the wall like a picture. A pair of these, hung on either side of the bathroom mirror, will give a touch of baronial hunting-lodge splendor to your bathroom.

Your ferns will do well if you place them on gravel-filled saucers holding water, in order to insure a moist but not wet condition. An occasional syringing or gentle splash in the shower will dislodge unwelcome insect pests, and will refresh your ferns immensely.

The third horizontal surface available, unless your bathroom is exceptionally spacious, is the toilet-tank top. Approach this fixture boldly. The ridiculous thing exists, so why not make a strong statement about it? Sweep away those back issues of *Mechanix Illustrated* and make room for the greenery. One approach is to place the plants directly on the tank

Construct the tray so that its bottom is above high-water mark.

top. Another is to remove the top entirely and set the plants within the tank in a homemade tray. Nail some 1 x 4 pieces of redwood together so that they form a rectangular tray that fits snugly inside the tank top. Tack strips of metal lathe across the bottom of the tray to help support the weight of the plant pots. Strips of molding tacked to the outside of the tray then rest on the top edge of the tank top, suspending the tray at the proper height. (Be sure to leave room below for the tank's internal works to function.) This installation looks more permanent and offers humidity-loving plants a fine source of moisture-laden air. If you have enough room, you can place plants in back and on the sides of the toilet. The wall space over the tank is ideal for hanging plants as well.

### Hanging Plants Use Little Space

Any vertical space in the bathroom, where your head doesn't ordinarily go, is potential space for a hanging plant. In order that you don't hang one where you will be constantly bumping into it, spend a little time analyzing the traffic pattern of the room. Walk through a typical morning bathroom ritual, several times, and have the other members of the family do the same. Note the areas that are out of the way of heads, elbows, and tossed towels. Then measure these spaces to determine the size of the plants that will go there. You'll probably find that the areas close to walls and the toilet are fairly free of traffic problems. Corners will probably furnish space for hanging plants, and you'll discover that plants hanging over countertops take up no work area at all. Any of the hanging plants discussed previously in this chapter will be fine, providing that their light requirements are met.

### Odd Places for Plants

If you've got a free-standing sink, there's room beneath it for a plant or two. The shower is a possibility, too. Why not keep the curtain pulled back so that you can

**Take advantage of unused space over toilet.**

hang plants from the curtain rod? Well, when the shower is used the plants would have to be moved. Since this is the case, why not hang them right in the shower, high up and in the corner, out of the way? This way they can enjoy the hot, wet air. Just keep hot water from reaching them. Another idea for the shower is a high shelf along two walls. Ferns can go on top and brushes, soap balls, and back scrubbers can hang underneath. Good and sufficient light, however, could be a problem in the shower as well as in other out-of-the-way places in the bathroom. If you have enough ceiling height, you can install a false translucent ceiling which conceals fluorescent lighting. This will give you soft, uniformly intense light throughout the room. Light colored walls and ceiling will distribute available light and make the room look bigger, too. Another way to brighten things up is to have plenty of mirror area. Mirrors make the room look bigger and brighter and they reflect light into dark corners.

Top-floor apartment dwellers often have a skylight in their bathroom. A cloud of hanging plants can be suspended under the skylight in such a way so as to not block light from each other. You can also build a planter up inside the skylight well that will hold trailing plants like *Asparagus Sprengeri* or *A. plumosus*. This method offers the advantage of letting a maximum amount of light into the room.

**Skylight is an open invitation for hanging plants. Stagger their heights so that light isn't blocked.**

## The Powder Room

Unfortunately, the powder room doesn't offer the decorator with plants the same advantages that its big brother the bathroom does. Powder rooms are usually small, warm, dark, and stuffy. Don't despair, though. You can grow plants successfully here, too, although your choice will be limited.

Consider screening your powder-room window with plants as discussed earlier in this chapter. Window shelves will take up the least amount of precious room, and the plants discussed for the bathroom window would be appropriate.

Anything you can do to make the powder room lighter and brighter will help your plants. Light colored walls and ceiling, large expanses of mirrors, fluorescent lighting designed for plants as well as for people, will all greatly improve your choice of plant candidates and your chances of success with them here. Plants that can take a lot of punishment include aglaonema, aspidistra, the dracaenas, some of the dwarf-palms, philodendrons, and sansevierias. As mentioned previously, aglaonema, philodendron, syngonium, and tradescantia will grow in shallow water. So will *Dracaena Sanderiana*, ivy, and pieces of Hawaiian tree-fern. Just remember to add a bit of charcoal to each, for sweetening.

*Trevesia palmata*

# 9. Halls and Entranceways

Halls and entranceways are the means by which we get from one environment to another and are usually navigated quickly and without interest. Plants can bring these dreary stretches to life and can make the trip more pleasant by setting the stage for what is to be found in the next room.

Space is tight in halls and entranceways, so plants will have to occupy those areas not needed by people. Large plants can be included if their branching or foliage occurs above head height. *Dracaena Massangeana* canes are a good example of the type of plant which can be used. Given sufficient ceiling height, these plants can produce an arch of foliage which would be very pleasant to walk beneath.

**Tall *Dracaena Massangeana* canes bear their foliage up and out of the way, forming a leafy entrance arch.**

*Ficus nitida* can be purchased as "standards" (plants pruned and trained into tree forms). Podocarpus grows straight up in a relatively narrow form, and so does pleomele.

*Philodendron oxycardium*, the vigorously climbing vine, can be trained to frame doorways off the hall. This plant could also be trained onto an arbor built just inside the entrance door of your house. A similar effect is achieved by placing large plants to either side of the entrance to a room. Plants used in this way allow the person to move into the room gradually and to discover its contents little by little. The person is prevented from establishing an instantaneous, all-encompassing appraisal of the room and, because the decor is revealed gradually, approaches with a sense of pleasurable anticipation.

Doorways leading to rooms off a hallway can be decorated with plants in ways that will reflect the individual personalities of the persons who occupy the rooms (such as bedrooms), or that express the use to which the rooms are usually put (such as the kitchen or laundry room). Let the occupants of bedrooms decorate their own doorways. A recluse teen-ager might select a prickly cactus to stand guard outside the door. A sconce of African violets might reflect the dainty personality of a nine-year-old girl, a staghorn-fern the heroic dreams of a twelve-year old boy. Of course, selection of plants depends a great deal upon the amount of available light. In halls and entranceways, supplemental lighting might be called for.

The wall at the end of a long hallway is a perfect place for a specimen plant. At its entrance, the hallway becomes a frame for the plant, the long lines of the ceiling, walls, and floor leading in perspective to the plant. To heighten the frame effect, paint the walls white, as well as the ceiling. Carpet the floor in white, if you've got the courage. Paint the far wall, against which the plant stands, a different color, but one complementary to the foliage of the plant.

Two *Ficus nitida* plants soften the entrance to this living room. The foliage serves to focus attention to the entranceway first, gradually yielding to inspection of the details of the room beyond.

Bedroom occupants express their personalities through plant decorations at their doorways. Watch out for cactus fanciers! Supplemental lighting is necessary in enclosed hallways.

*Dracaena Sanderiana*

# 10. The City Apartment

Plants in the city aren't a luxury, they are necessary items of survival gear in the dark, dirty, depersonalized environments offered by our large urban areas. Don't be afraid to grow plants in the city. Like humans, they need a bit more attention in order to flourish in this alien environment; and if you know what the problems are, you can take steps to overcome them.

The major difficulties you will encounter are reduced natural light, because of the lack of window area and blockages caused by other buildings, and an overly dry interior atmosphere, caused by steam heat and lack of proper ventilation. Artificial lighting can solve some of your natural-illumination problems, particularly in small rooms like kitchens and bathrooms, which are likely to have no windows at all. But in the living room and bedroom, the careful selection of the right plants can overcome most light problems.

Plants with large, smooth, glossy leaves are the best bets for city apartments. They are easy to swab down occasionally, and a weekly sponging will open clogged leaf pores and dislodge insect pests and their eggs. Also, this type of plant is usually indigenous to the tropical forest, where it has developed a tolerance for dim light. The philodendrons fall into this category and offer a number of leaf shapes and plant forms that have

**Light floods into most top-floor city apartments. Plants soak up the sun during the day and then move into the room, as accents and area definers, at night. Set the plant tubs on casters for easy mobility.**

been discussed previously. This useful and inexpensive plant will survive the most adverse conditions and is recommended for dimly lit rooms and hallways.

Many of the palms tolerate low light levels. The howea, or kentia, palm is particularly invulnerable to dim light, and is so popular that it is often difficult to find in large sizes. The bamboo and areca palms offer interesting alternatives. *Phoenix Roebelenii*, the date-palm, and the rhapis palm want more light. *Chamaerops humilis*, the fan-palm, needs sun.

The dracaenas are good city dwellers. The smaller varieties, *D. Godseffiana*, *D. Sanderiana*, and *D. Warneckii*, tolerate surprisingly low light levels. *Dracaena Massangeana* bears tufts of corn-plant-shaped and -colored leaves at the end of sturdy canes. Give it medium light, as you do *D. marginata*, its more feathery-leaved relative.

A mirror at the back of this three-story outdoor greenhouse increases the apparent size of the ten-foot depth. The plants were selected for their tolerance for low light. *Dracaena Massangeana*, philodendron, dieffenbachia, varieties of ficus, and a staghorn-fern are reported to be alive and well.

Dieffenbachia is a rewarding city plant which tolerates low humidity. It is available in sizes ranging from small on up to four-foot specimens. Although their leaves are large, dieffenbachias are so delicately shaped in·tones of yellow-green through lime-green that they do not overpower their surroundings. These plants make splendid companions for antique furniture of almost any vintage and for stone and marble sculpture.

It's always a great temptation to grow ferns, especially since they look so healthy in the greenhouse. But because of their humidity requirements, ferns can be a disappointment in the city apartments. If your window exposure seems ideal for ferns and you are willing to take the chance, build a water and pebble tray for them so that the humidity is raised in their immediate area. Then see to it that proper ventilation is maintained by regularly opening a window in another room. In addition, spray your ferns regularly with a mist of water to keep that humidity high. Often a fern will decide that it likes its environment, for some unexplainable reason, and it will thrive. Maybe you'll be lucky.

*Asplenium Nidus*, the bird's-nest fern, tolerates low light levels. It has unusual, lime-green, broad-leaved foliage. The old-fashioned Boston fern and some of its fluffy and ruffled cousins need more light and humidity.

The ficus family offers several city-tolerant candidates. *Ficus nitida* and *F. benjamina* want good light and reward

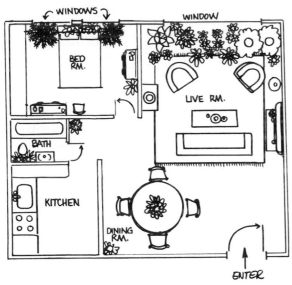

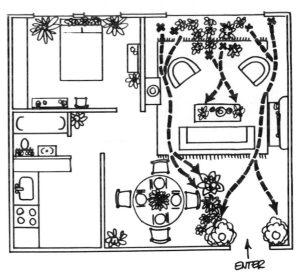

A. Daytime

B. Guests about to arrive

your thoughtful treatment with glossy, lime-green leaves and a graceful, contemporary growth habit. Caution: these particular ficus are touchy about being moved from location to location and can lose much of their foliage (temporarily, except in extreme cases) if exposed to drastic changes in temperature and ventilation. *Ficus elastica* and *F. lyrata*, the familiar rubber-plant and fiddle-leaf fig, both tolerate medium light. The tree form of *F. elastica* is striking, if the room is large enough to carry it. *F. lyrata* is more open and free-form, although it grows every bit as large.

Brassaia, or schefflera, is much used in urban commercial installations. In New York City, this plant, along with philodendrons of all kinds, ficus, and other tropicals, is used outdoors in display plantings in front of many of the newer buildings in midtown. They seem to do very well and respond to frequent hosings to wash off soot and dirt with vigorous growth. These plants are removed, of course, when frost approaches, and are set out again the following May. In apartments, keep brassaia out of the direct sun, as it is known to scorch.

Large plants should be placed on platforms fitted with casters so that you can move them as the spirit moves you.

There's no horticultural reason to keep plants near the window after dark, and in cramped space plants should serve multiple purposes. Shift them into the room at night and create intimate conversation and dining areas.

Imagine that you are giving an important dinner party in your stunningly decorated (but small) apartment. Your plant inventory consists of two tall and beautiful *Ficus nitida* which usually stand on either side of the large window (the only source of natural light in the room), a pair of tall brassaia, some medium-sized *Ficus lyrata* and dieffenbachia, and some small flowering plants—begonias, some bromeliads, and geraniums. Just before the first guest arrives, you roll the pair of ficus plants over to the front door and place them at either side of the entrance, so that they create the effect of coming into the apartment through a garden bower. Next, you trundle the brassaia over to the dining area and place them so as to keep the secret of your elegantly set dining table . . . at least until dinnertime. Then you place the dieffenbachia and fiddle-leaf fig plants at strategic locations within the room where they help to define conversation areas and to add detail and interest to your room while enhancing the party atmosphere. Finally,

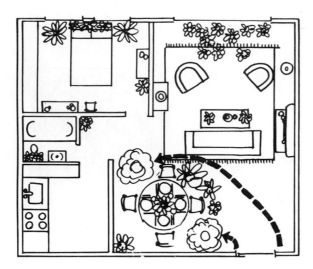

**C. Dinnertime**

you distribute your flowering plants among the nuts, crackers, and onion dips on the coffee table and occasional tables.

Now it is time for dinner to be served. After everyone has been seated, and the roast has been presented, it only remains for you to pull over those two ficus trees guarding the door to join the brassaia in enclosing your dining area in intimate greenery. Next morning, with the praises of your guests still in your ears, everything is maneuvered back to its usual source of daylight.

Tiny apartment bedrooms can be made brighter and will appear to be larger, if mirrors are used along with plants, a device demonstrated before in the chapters on both the living room and the bedroom. A large floor-to-ceiling mirror can work with carefully placed plants to create the illusion of a doorway into a tropical conservatory, angling the glass slightly so as to not reflect the viewer or furniture from the point of view of the person lying in bed. The edges of the mirror are disguised by plants or draperies. Waking up to this feeling of space is especially nice in the confines of city living.

An herb garden is a delight, and no city kitchen should be without one. Sunny kitchen windows are hard to come by, but fluorescent fixtures and special plant tubes allow fresh herbs to prosper in the darkest of corners. See the section on light, in Chapter 13, Plant Care, for directions on building or buying an artificially illuminated plant garden. Try your hand at African violets, too, if you've got the space.

A lot of the top-floor apartments in old New York brownstones have skylights in the bathrooms. These are usually tunnels about two feet square running from the ceiling to the roof and capped with a glass and steel "light." Hanging plant baskets can be suspended in the light tunnel. A pulley arrangement can be added to lower the plants for watering. Larger skylights offer the opportunity to build a planter around their sides. Depending upon the light admitted, hanging plants of numerous varieties could be planted to frame the skylight. Planters located out of reach are often forgotten and are allowed to dry out, so be careful.

### Summer Camp for Apartment Plants

During the warm late spring, summer, and early fall months, most houseplants will get a new lease on life if allowed to remain out of doors on the terrace, rooftop, fire escape, or what-have-you. Exceptions are the gesneriads (African violets,

**Protect plants from wind and scorching sun. Anchor container bases securely. Plunge small containers into moisture-retentive medium (shredded Sunday *Times*). Water often, syringing fallout from leaves.**

City apartment: A magnificent staghorn-fern keeps an eye
on things in this New York walkup apartment. A Boston fern
and several orchids hang at the windows. Spring-flowering
bulbs, some potted azaleas, a Rex begonia, and cut flowers
bring the sunshine right inside.

The definitive office garden: The interior of the
Ford Foundation building in New York City is
a gigantic greenhouse. The offices face this
interior courtyard rather than the city outside.
Giant magnolias, ferns, Japanese holly,
azaleas, poinsettias (and other seasonal
flowers) keep workers smiling.

Mirrored walls expand and bend space, corners disappear,
and you are left surrounded by light and green. Baskets of
cissus hang at the windows and ferns luxuriate beneath—
among them a magnificent bird's-nest variety.

**Entranceway:** In this ground-floor entrance to a New York brownstone, light is supplied by fluorescent tubing hidden behind walls and ceiling of polyethylene film. The tiny stream and waterfall add constant humidity to the air.

gloxinias, etc.) whose hairy leaves and delicate flowers are no match for air pollution and sooty fallout.

Medium-sized and tall plants are usually planted in large enough tubs so that drying out between waterings or rains isn't usually a problem. Small plants should be plunged, with their pots, into larger containers containing soil, peat moss, or other moisture-retentive material (sawdust, perlite, packing fiber, even shredded newspapers).

Make sure that the outdoor spot each houseplant occupies offers the same light intensity (or close to it) that is called for in interior use. Philodendrons will scorch in blazing sun, and succulents will not be happy for long in deep shade. Make allowance for wind by bracing plants securely. Often containers that are appropriate for indoor use don't offer sufficient base weight to offset the leverage exerted by wind against a large leaf mass.

The tiniest terrace, or even the fire escape, can provide an interesting decorating device while offering plants relief from the stuffy indoors. Place your large plants on the terrace so that they can be seen from inside the apartment. They should flank the window and be placed

The tiny backyard of this New York brownstone was enclosed by a greenhouselike structure and turned into a lush, year-round living area. Artificial lighting supplements dim fare received by most New York backyards. Dieffenbachia, dracaena, spathiphyllum, ficus, palms, and other tried-and-true city dwellers flourish.

far enough out so that smaller plants can be placed in front of them. Match these large plants with additional varieties on the inside of the room. Place medium-sized and small plants both outside and inside so that the talls frame the mediums and the mediums frame the smalls. The effect will expand the apparent size of the room. Periodically rotate the plants so that all receive a taste of the great outdoors.

Increase the effectiveness of your indoor-outdoor display by running an all-weather extension cord out the window and hooking up a couple of weatherproof spotlights. The effect at night will delight you, especially when all of the interior lights are turned off.

Plants furnish better late-night viewing than most TV fare. Plants are outside on the fire escape; lighting dramatizes their presence.

aphelandra

# II. The Office

Office workers, from file clerks to executives, spend the most demanding hours of the day in an enclosed and often hectic environment. They need all the help they can get ( I know, I used to be one), and plants make natural and restful companions during those long stretches from nine to five.

Today's office buildings are almost all air-conditioned and plants adapt almost as readily to this innovation as people. Air conditioning keeps the temperature at an even level, and because windows in modern buildings are not made to open easily, drafts are avoided. On weekends, when air conditioning is usually shut down, you can provide additional moisture so that the plants won't suffer from the increased temperature and stuffy atmosphere. Group the plants together so that they benefit from one another's transpiration process. In addition, place a pan of water under or near the plants so that water vapor will be constantly added to the air.

Sufficient light is rarely a problem in offices, even if yours has no windows. Overhead fluorescent lights furnish sufficient illumination to at least keep low-light-tolerant plants happy. Over weekends, when the lights are off, plants will receive less light than they require, however. If possible, on Mondays place your plants near a bright light source so that they can be rejuvenated after their dull weekend.

Office workers who are about to go on vacation are advised to distribute their plants among friends who will keep them watered. This is better than keeping your plants in your own office and exacting a promise to care for them from someone. That person could forget or be absent for days with an illness.

As in any room, plants in the office will do best when grouped together. If you are placing plants on a windowsill, check to see if the heating ductwork runs underneath (it does in most modern buildings). You can place a piece of asbestos on the sill to protect your plants from the heat.

The water-pebble tray is always a good idea for maintaining high humidity around your plants (see "Moisture" in Chapter 13, Plant Care). A small humidifier will work wonders for your plants, and for you, too. Automatic timers are inexpensive and will turn your humidifier on and off according to your setting. Automatic humidity control will assure your plants of adequate moisture over the weekends. It's also a good idea to keep some sort of spritzing contraption handy and full of water. Frequent foggings will keep foliage clean and the humidity up.

Windows that receive even a small amount of direct sun will become too hot for plants during the period of ex-

Check windowsill for overheating caused by radiator or ductwork. Sheets of asbestos should be placed beneath plant tray for insulation. Sunny windows need blinds for hottest part of the day.

Architects Stanley and Laurie Maurer have set aside a work area in their remodeled Brooklyn townhouse. Assorted ferns, small palms, ivy, chlorophytum, and hoya bask in the brilliant light reflected from the white walls. Notice that plants occupy their space, people theirs. Maurers keep small sprayers handy for constant spritzing of plant foliage. Humidity stays high, plants love it.

posure, unless you provide screening or filtering. Venetian blinds and draperies should be drawn during periods of intense sun. If no such protection is available, place your plants far enough away from the window to safeguard against scorching.

## Plants for Sunny Offices

Most flowering plants demand a certain amount of direct sunlight in order to produce blooms. But prolonged and unfiltered exposure to the direct rays of the sun can be harmful to even these plants. Be sure to follow the suggestions above.

Gardenias, any of the citrus plants, crotons, kalanchoë, and geraniums all thrive in full sun. So do any of the cactus varieties, and the sunny window ledge is a perfect spot for a well-designed cactus

tray. Keep tulips, hyacinths, daffodils, and lilies in the sun until the flower buds begin to show color. Then move them to a cooler, less bright location in order to prolong their bloom.

Plants in direct sun will dry out quickly, so keep the blinds drawn over the weekend unless you've devised a method of automatic watering. Moving your plants to a less evaporation-prone position is a good idea, too. Of course, a water-pebble tray should be filled every day, and particularly on Friday evening just before quitting time.

## Plants for Shady Offices

Overhead fluorescent lighting is left on all day long in most big city offices, so even the dullest windows can support a wealth of plants.

In general, plants which require medium light can be maintained in any office with windows, plus supplemental lighting from the illumination system of the building. In this group are anthurium, aspidistra, many of the ferns including *Asplenium Nidus* and nephrolepis, azaleas, begonias, bromeliads, caladiums, several palms—including areca, *Neanthe bella*, howea, bamboo, phoenix, and rhapis— kangaroo-vine, grape-ivy, dieffenbachia, the dracaenas, *Ficus elastica* and *F. pandurata*, schefflera, and more.

Flowering bulbs will brighten the shady office, providing they have been allowed to develop their buds in a sunny location. They will actually remain in flower longer in the shady office, and when their flowers are finished their foliage remains attractive for a while. Take them home when the leaves begin to yellow and plant them out of doors to ripen off.

There is less danger of plants drying out in the shady office. But overwatering can be almost as big a problem, particularly if an overindulgent or misinformed secretary is attending to the watering. Remember the rule of thumb: if the soil is moist to the touch, the plant has sufficient water.

Subirrigation will eliminate the problem of watering and will assure an adequate supply of moisure over weekends and holidays. Directions for applying this method are also given in the section on moisture in the chapter on plant care. The water-pebble tray should be considered, too, if you are grouping your plants. You'll find directions for its construction and use in the same section.

Illustrator Tim Shortt is an avid office gardener who maintains a homey jumble of assorted pots, bowls, plastic cups, and cooky tins filled with an equally disparate collection of plants. He keeps his horticultural zoo on the shelf in front of the window, which he pries open for ventilation on nice days.

While at his drawing board one day, Tim was suddenly overcome by a great sense of personal loss. Glancing at the window, he saw a large gap where his

Pittosporum gains temporary respite from humdrum office routine.

favorite three-foot pittosporum usually stood. Upon looking out the window, he saw to his horror that it was now gracing the roof of a building six stories below. The plant was retrieved, more or less intact, having parted company with its pot on the way down, which allowed the foliage to act as a parachute. It is now back among its friends and seems to have recovered from the trip, except for the shape of its leaves. They insist on curling under at the edges, as if they are clutching for some invisible means of support.

### Windowless Offices, Cubicles, and Cubbyholes

The smaller the space you occupy at the office, the more you want to express your own personality and individuality.

Tropical plants cover a wide range of light-level tolerance. Philodendrons occupy dimmer areas, while flowering plants bask in bright light at the window.

Plants can take away the cramped feeling of a small space and even seem to expand it. But most importantly, plants welcome you to work each morning and greet each visitor to your desk during the day.

Overhead fluorescent lighting should insure enough illumination to grow many of the low-light-tolerant plants. These include aspidistra, aglaonema (which can be grown, without soil, in a vase of water), several of the palms and dracaenas, and some of the ferns. The philodendrons are used to low light but many of them have large leaves which might overpower a small space. An exception is the ubiquitous *Philodendron cordatum*, whose small, heart-shaped leaves are borne on fast-growing, vining stems. You can train it to climb on strings or wires, so that a desk next to a wall or partition can boast a background of shiny green leaves. Sansevieria and spathiphyllum should also do well even though the light level is low.

If you've got room on your desk, or on a nearby bookcase or file cabinet, you can maintain a small, artificially lit garden of flowering plants. All you need is one of the many kinds of commercially produced fluorescent light stands made especially for growing saintpaulias, gloxinias, herbs, etc. The larger plant markets often carry a selection of these stands.

Terrariums bring a moist, woodsy, mysterious world to your otherwise businesslike desktop. You can buy ready-made terrariums or you can make your own (Chapter 12, Containers, tells you how). Make sure that you use plants adapted for low light. Immature specimens of the plants listed above are good bets. So are peperomia, syngonium, acorus, and haworthia. Try some of the small-leaved ivies, too.

A rectangular aquarium will act like a terrarium while supporting a more varied landscape. You can combine miniature plants, rock outcroppings and mysterious caves, interesting twigs and bits of weathered driftwood, and mosses (a sensational tank garden can be made completely of different kinds of mosses which you've brought back from the country). Have some fun with your miniature garden and include some personal objects in the landscape. Bits of costume jewelry can substitute for rocks. Tiny plastic dinosaurs can do battle in a primeval swamp while toy cattle graze unconcernedly and peacefully nearby, and figures of friends cut out of photographs stroll among the ferns. A piece of window glass should cover the top of the tank in order to maintain the water recycling process. Leave an opening an inch or so wide at one end of the tank for ventilation.

# Part Three

# Keeping
# Your
# Plants
# Happy

*Dracaena Massangeana*

# 12. Containers

In decorating with plants, the container can often be as important a design element as the plant. Certainly the wrong size or shape, or an inappropriate decoration, can call undue attention to the container and diminish the impact of the plant.

Choose containers that form a visually balanced base for the plant. A too small container will make the plant look top-heavy. You will always feel slightly uncomfortable around this plant because you will be wondering when it will topple. On the other hand, too large a container will look dumpy and bottom-heavy, and its plant will appear undersized. Containers that taper can be larger than those with vertical sides. Cylinders can be taller than squares or rectangles.

When grouping containers and plants, give as much thought to the relationships among shapes as you do to the relationships among foliage colors, shapes, and textures. Avoid clumping containers of the same size and shape. Aim for visual interest, playing curves against angles, smooth surfaces against textured ones.

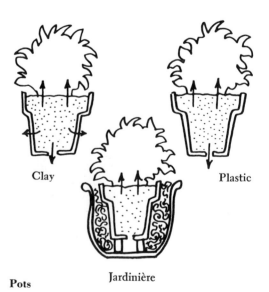

Clay

Plastic

Jardinière

Pots

Plants in pottery containers will require more frequent watering than those planted in plastic or metal containers. This is because pottery "breathes" through its sides, and moisture in the soil evaporates through these surfaces as well as through the open top. If too much evaporation occurs, the soil next to the inside surface of the container will shrink away from it, leaving a space. Then when you do water, the water will run down the insides of the container and out the drainage hole, without penetrating the soil to an effective depth. If this happens, soak the whole works in the tub until the soil becomes thoroughly saturated and once again swells against the sides of the pot. Because of the unequal evaporation rates of moisture in the soil contained in plastic, or other nonporous material, and pottery, it's a good idea not to combine the two materials in the same grouping.

The container may directly hold the soil and plant within it, or it may act as a jardinière, containing another pot which holds the soil and plant. Jardinières act as a reservoir for water draining from the inner container, so be careful to avoid overwatering. But jardinières also inhibit the loss of moisture through the sides of clay pots, especially if a layer of peat moss is placed as insulation between the two.

## Pottery

The first plant containers were probably made from clay, and today this warm, earthy material is still much loved.

The florist's simple clay flowerpot is a classic design. A cluster of these in different sizes can be striking.

Italian pottery is ornate and elegant. Bearing names such as *Casetta Festonata* and *Triangolo di Frutta*, these earthy but regal urns, shells, squares, and rounds are festooned with garlands of fruit and flowers, flights of cherubs, and prancing satyrs and lions. In the right setting, these containers are knockouts.

Contemporary craftsmen and designers are still working in pottery, creating simplified shapes and textures. These containers depend on their crisp, geo-

Pottery containers come in many sizes, shapes, and textures. Styles range from ancient to contemporary.

metric shapes and the perfection of line and form for their interest. Most of them are devoid of ornamentation except for some with simple, finely detailed texturing. Colors range from white through the many glazes, including sienna yellow, the ochers, rusts, dark olives, purples, blues, and flame glazes.

In the southwestern parts of the United States much Indian and Mexican pottery is seen. These beautifully decorated and glazed pots make perfect containers for cactus and other succulents as well as for palms and dracaenas.

## Plastics

Aside from the florist's plastic flowerpot, which has great utility but little loveliness, plastic containers can be quite handsome (although expensive).

Fiber-glass containers are manufactured in increasing quantities, and as competition between manufacturers increases, prices are becoming more reasonable and new and beautiful designs are appearing. Shapes run a wide range, from cylinders, squares, and rectangles through

flared, tapered, concave, and convex variations on these themes. Lyrical curvilinear shapes are also available. Any color can be had, in a matte, glossy, or textured finish. Fiber-glass containers stand all kinds of weather and can be used outdoors anywhere.

Clear plastic cylinders, available in a variety of diameters, can be bought at plastic-supply houses. The material is easy

Unusual shapes, impossible to achieve in pottery, are available in fiber glass.

131

to cut, glue, and polish, and many unusual and striking containers can be made from it.

Using plastic cement, attach a clear plastic disk one-third of the way down inside a cylinder which you've cut to the desired height. When the connection is dry, place a two-inch layer of coarse gravel or pebbles on the disk, then a layer of fine gravel, and finally rich, brown potting soil and an appropriate plant. Now sit back and watch as the roots develop and push through the soil. Be careful in watering! Add a little at a time until water covers the layer of coarse gravel. Group several of these cylinders whose interior bases are glued on at different heights.

Flat sheets of acrylic can be cut to size and glued together to form squares or rectangles. By gluing a base piece at some interior point, planters similar in concept to the cylinders described above can be constructed. Acrylic comes in colors, too, and the vivid hues are well suited to complementing plants.

Clear acrylic domes make great hanging baskets. Drill holes in the lip (at least three), through which you will later string the supporting wires, thongs, ropes, nylon line, or whatever. (See page 59.) Build up the planting medium from a two-inch layer of coarse gravel or pebbles, then finer gravel, then a layer of crushed charcoal for sweetening, and finally the deep, dark soil mixture. Water carefully so that water does not collect above the layer of coarse gravel.

### Containers from the Brickyard

Brickyards, stone yards, or lumberyards which stock these materials usually carry a complete line of clay drainage pipes and fittings, round or square chimney flues, and decorative clay chimney pots. The simple shapes and handsome terra-cotta color of these materials make them useful as plant containers at home.

Shapes run to round, rectangular, and octagonal. Lengths vary, but you can easily cut them to size, using a masonry blade and an electric saw. Pieces of pipe

can be glued together with epoxy cement to form interesting constructions. Pieces of marine plywood, glued to the base with epoxy cement, will make any pipe into a waterproof container (remember to drill a drainage hole in the plywood).

Pipe fittings are used by engineers to join lengths of pipe together in various ways. They come in a wealth of interesting shapes that make them striking pieces of sculpture as well as efficient plant containers. Junction pipes can be hung from wires, cords, or thongs, with plants peeping from their oddly angled orifices. The holes are stopped with half disks of plywood, glued with epoxy cement.

**Building-supply yards yield all kinds of interestingly shaped potential plant containers. Here, drainage pipes and chimney pots.**

Featherock is easily worked, using a chisel and mallet to chip out a basin for holding the soil. It's to be used like a flowerpot, so drill a drainage hole through the rock with a masonry bit and electric drill. Featherock is sharp! Wear gloves.

Flue pipes are found in sizes ranging from six inches in diameter up to three feet. Lengths are usually standard at two feet, a fortunate height for a container holding a large plant. Shapes are round and rectangular.

Chimney pots seem to be right out of Charles Dickens' London. They range in size from a foot to three feet high and their somewhat gothic sculpting makes them interesting bases for large, spreading ferns or for hanging baskets of ivy.

### Rock Containers (Natural and Artificial)

A naturally hollowed-out rock will support soil and plants as well as any man-made container, provided that a hole is drilled through for drainage. No drainage hole is required if you are growing moss or succulents, but careful watering is a must.

Featherock is a lightweight stone, the end product of lava flows that cooled thousands of years ago in the Sierra Nevada Mountains. Featherock is one-fifth the weight of ordinary boulders of comparable size and is chemically neutral. It can be easily cut, shaped, hollowed out, and drilled. Colors are silver gray, char-

coal, and tan. Caution: always use gloves when handling featherock; its surface is sharp!

Select a featherock boulder to be used for a plant container and smooth its base with a rasp file until it sits securely on the floor. Next, chop out a basin, using a carpenter's hatchet for the rough work and finishing off the hole with a hammer and chisel. Bore a hole for drainage, using an electric drill and a masonry bit. Plant in your featherock container as you would in any other pot, building up from coarse gravel to the soil mix.

Large planters faced with stone can be built where a permanent grouping of large plants is wanted. Because of the weight of stone, flooring will have to be supported from below unless the floor is on a concrete slab.

The first step is to build a wooden frame which will hold the plants and support the stone veneer. Make sure that the frame is securely attached to the floor so that sudden jolts will not crack the cement mortar you will be using.

A waterproof lining must now be attached to the inside of the frame. Copper or stainless steel is the best material for the lining and it can be made to order

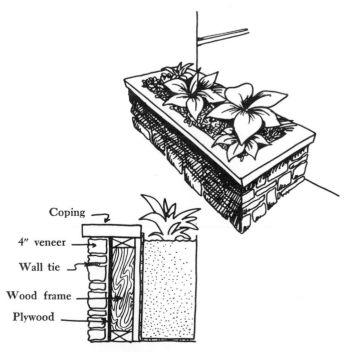

Coping

4″ veneer

Wall tie

Wood frame

Plywood

A stone veneer over a wooden frame is lighter than solid stone, but check your floor construction and add support below if necessary.

by a metalworking shop. A marine-plywood lining can be built at home providing it can be made absolutely watertight. Epoxy glue should do the trick, although a layer of fiber glass and epoxy resin would be better.

Pitch the bottom of the liner slightly, so that water will run to one end. At this end, allow for drainage by inserting a piece of copper tubing which will run through a hole in the baseboard and on down into the basement. If the planter is built on a concrete slab, with no basement under it, attach a petcock to the end of the copper tubing so that the planter can be drained into a bucket after heavy waterings.

After the frame is built and lined, cover the outside with plywood or plasterboard or Masonite. This backing is necessary so that the stone facing can be securely mortared to it.

A mortar mix of one part cement and three parts sand should be mixed with water to a workable consistency. Individual stones can now be laid up. Don't set them on end, or in other unnatural positions, and don't set stones of the same size and shape next to each other. Make joints approximately one-half inch wide and fill completely with mortar. Pack the space between the stones and the backing with mortar. When you've laid several stones, clean out their joints with a stick or a dull point. Be sure to brush off all excess mortar before it sets. For a strong wall, bond the stone to the frame with metal wall ties. These are nailed to the backing and are caught between the stones as they are laid up.

Finally, a coping stone finishes off the top of the stonework and hides the wooden frame. These coping stones can be cut to size at the yard where you buy them. Attach the coping stones with epoxy; your stone dealer will sell you the the proper materials.

The stone used above can be standard four-inch stone where weight is not a problem (forty square feet of this material weighs one ton). Where weight must be kept to a minimum, a special one-inch veneering stone is available.

These stones are grooved top and bottom in order to receive metal clips which are screwed into the backing. After the stone veneer is in place, held by the metal clips, the joints are filled in with mortar.

Artificial-boulder containers can be made from a mixture of cement and several lightening ingredients. Combine one part Portland cement with one and a half parts coarse perlite and one and a half parts shredded sphagnum peat moss. Combine thoroughly before adding any water. When the mixture is wet, aim for a consistency that is not sloppy but which will stick together when patted onto a mold. When the mix is just right, add coloring before molding. Coloring will come dry, a limeproof powder in black, burnt umber, raw sienna and burnt sienna, Venetian red, ocher, blue, green, and vermilion. Do some test runs, using colors in various combinations, before you tackle the finished product.

To make your form: 1. Turn kitchen bowls of different sizes upside down, and pack damp sand over them. 2. Shape a chicken-wire armature over the sand (being careful not to disturb it). Remove the formed armature for future use.

3. Next, build a dam of more sand around the base of the sand mold, about an inch away from it, and 4., spread a sheet of plastic (the kind the cleaner sends your garments home in) over the mold. Press the plastic into the moat and over the lip of the dam.

5. Now make your concrete mixture and trowel it on, filling in the moat formed by the dam, and covering the entire mold with a layer about one-half inch thick. Place the chicken-wire armature over the whole form, pressing it into the wet concrete. Spread another half inch of concrete over the chicken wire, making sure that it is pressed well into the mesh of the wire.

6. Drainage holes are formed by pushing wooden dowels through the bottom of the container. Make sure that the dowels pass through the wire mesh and make contact with the plastic.

7. After twelve hours, the cement should be hard enough to allow removal

**Making an artificial-boulder container**

Using a folded-paper funnel, pour fine gravel into the bottom of your glass container. The depth of the gravel should range from a quarter of an inch in small bottles to several inches in larger ones. Shake the container in order to distribute the gravel evenly. Next, funnel in a layer of crushed charcoal (for sweetening), and an inch or two of pasteurized or inert soil mix (more for larger containers, less for small ones). Push the soil around into the desired hills and valleys, using a small long-handled shovel. Now add your rocks, pieces of driftwood, and other non-growing elements. Long-handled tweezers and tampers will come in handy here.

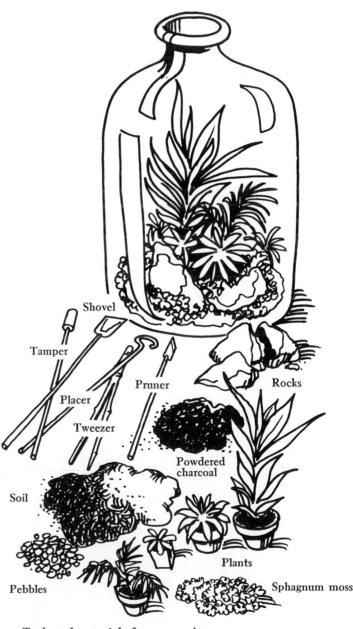

**Tools and materials for a terrarium**

of the dowels. Also at this time, level off the bottom of the container by scraping away the still-workable cement with a piece of straight-edged glass. Texture the concrete if you wish, using a wire brush.

8. When the container is completely dry, soak it in water, which is changed every two days, for two weeks. This process leaches out the lime. Another way to do it is to leave the container outside for a month or so. If it picks up a coating of moss or algae, so much the better.

9. After your artificial-boulder container has cured, plant it using methods recommended for other containers.

### Terrariums

Almost any glass container will do for a terrarium as long as the glass is clear enough to admit sufficient light. Brandy snifters, demijohns, fish tanks, large water-cooler jugs, and clear electric-light globes all make good terrariums.

**Terrariums can be planted in clear containers of all sorts of sizes and shapes.**

Remove plants from their pots and cut away one-third of their root systems and adhering soil. Place the plants in position in the terrarium, using a long-handled open-ended wide loop. Shovel soil little by little, until the roots are covered. After all the plants, rocks, and other items are in place, settle the soil by careful wetting. There is no drain for excess water in a terrarium, so be careful to avoid creating a boggy condition. Use an eyedropper or syringe, and make sure that accumulated water doesn't rise above the level of the drainage material.

Cover the completed terrarium and let it stand overnight. In the morning check to see if the surface of the soil is dry. It it is, add more water. If droplets of water have collected on the glass, the soil is too wet, and you should leave the cover off for a day. Repeat these checks and steps until a balance is achieved, that is, when a light coating of vapor appears on the glass at night.

When in balance, terrariums will need no attention for months. If plants grow too rampantly, cut them back with a long-handled pruner (an X-Acto blade

attached to a long dowel). Dead or unsightly plants can be removed and replaced.

Peperomia, haworthia, euonymus, many of the ferns, ivy, cryptanthus, columnea, and maranta are just a few of the traditional terrarium plants for you to choose from. For larger terrariums, look to spathiphyllum, aglaonema, aspidistra, and dieffenbachia. Many plants will flower if exposed to long enough periods of natural or artificial light. These include small-leaved begonias, columnea, saintpaulia, streptocarpus, and others, including several miniature species of orchid.

### Saikei or Tray Landscapes

Saikei (pronounced sigh-kay), like bonsai, is an art that was developed in Japan. Saikei emphasizes rock and groves of trees to give the effect of craggy landscapes and coastal headlands. The Japanese often add tiny porcelain figures of people and animals, boats, bridges, and houses. But you could substitute personal objects such as toy tractors and trucks, toy soldiers, cutout photos of members of the family (glued to stiff cardboard so that they stand up), baubles of costume jewelry, or what have you. As long as all of the elements are in scale with each other, your saikei can be any size you wish—right on up to room size.

Traditional saikei methods call for the dwarfing and training of trees, as in bonsai. You can buy trees which have been so treated, or you can hunt around for suitably shaped, small tropical houseplants. *Polyscias fruticosa*, the ming-tree, has a delicate branching structure and finely cut leaves. *Dizygotheca elegantissima*, or aralia, is another good one. Small podocarpus and areca palms are good because of their nicely scaled foliage. *Crassula argentea*, or Chinese jade, would work well with carefully selected rocks. Several of the small-leaved varieties of ivy are excellent, like *Cissus rhombifolia*, or grape-ivy. Within the geranium family are many plants that can be trained to bonsai-like forms. Herbal plants such as rose-

**Frank Okamura has been with the Brooklyn Botanical Garden since 1947. Besides overseeing the landscape operations on their famous Japanese gardens, Mr. Okamura is in charge of the Botanical Garden's vases and valuable collection of bonsai and saikei.**

mary, salvia, and lavender-cotton are good bets. Acacias, camellias, fuchsias, and lantanas will work in saikei, as will *Gardenia radicans*, *Ficus diversifolia*, and *Osmanthus fragrans*, or sweet-olive. Grapefruit has been used successfully, and so have some of the dwarf bamboos.

Traditional saikei trays can be bought, and so can flat bonsai pottery. If you can't find what you want, build a tray yourself. Waterproof plywood will do for the base and sides. Make it watertight with epoxy cement. Or use heavier wood and sand down the sides into gently undulating waves with a belt sander. An excellent saikei tray can be made using the method described earlier in this chapter for building artificial-rock containers. Traditional Japanese measurements call for the sides to be one-third as high as the length and the width two-thirds of the length.

Saikei trays must have drainage holes. Cover these with bits of broken pottery or use squares of aluminum screening (1.). Cut screening at least an inch larger all around than the hole. Press the screening into the hole with your finger, and secure it on the other side by passing a piece of copper wire through it where it pokes through the underside of the tray.

Place an inch or so of pebbles on the bottom of the tray. Cover these with a piece of fiber-glass cloth, or some fiber-glass insulation, in order to keep the soil and the gravel separated (soil seeping down through the drainage holes makes a mess). Next, spread on a half-inch layer of soil mix. Then (2.), place your major rocks and other nongrowing features, and position your plants, placing them on cones of soil in order to establish their proper heights. Finally, add the rest of the soil (3.), settling it gently around the roots with carefully sprinkled water. Create the topography of your saikei (4.) as you go along.

The health of your saikei landscape will depend in large part upon the rapid movement of air and water through the soil, so be sure you take the time to insure that your drainage system is working

**Building the saikei landscape**

A simple cube jardinière, constructed from cardboard and packing tape, can be decorated as whimsically or as seriously as you're in the mood for.

properly. Avoid overfeeding, since undue growth stimulation will lead to an unattractive, ragged appearance and a loss of overall scale.

Cactus adapts beautifully to tray gardens. Holes won't be necessary in the cactus tray, but you must fill the bottom with a layer of grit or gravel at least one and a half inches thick. You will maintain water in this layer to a depth of one and a quarter inches, except in winter (see page 162). On top of the gravel, place a mixture of two parts loam, one part peat moss, one part washed sand, one-half part bone meal, and one-half part rotted and shredded manure. This mixture should be two and one-half inches deep. After you have planted your cacti, cover the landscape with a quarter of an inch of aquarium gravel, or whatever else is appropriate to your decorative scheme.

### Quick and Unusual Effects

If you like to change your decorating schemes frequently, there's no need to lock yourself into a specific container style. Keep the plant in the pot it came in and use a larger, expendable container to mask it. The outer container can be of almost any material, even cardboard, since it will not be in contact with mois-

ture. Cardboard packing cylinders can be sawn to the desired lengths, and cardboard boxes can be reinforced with tape prior to decorating the surfaces.

Some ideas:

Cover the boxes or cylinders with wallpaper that matches the walls.

Cover them with matching drapery or slipcover fabric.

Cover them with brightly colored felt or burlap.

Glue on sheets of tiny mirrors for a gleaming, faceted effect.

Paste on a collage of family photographs, or magazine cutouts. Have giant enlargements made of favorite photos and glue them on the boxes.

Cover the boxes with carpeting (try AstroTurf).

Paint the containers in exciting colors or designs, such as a worm's-eye view of the root system and surrounding soil.

Exterior containers can be built from interesting woods, such as paneling or weathered barn wood. Sheets of wood veneer can be glued to boxes and cylinders.

A favorite piece of driftwood can be hollowed out to receive a plant and its pot.

Grass matting can be glued on the boxes. So can strips of bamboo.

**schefflera**

# 13. Plant Care

## TEMPERATURE

When we think of the tropics, we imagine a steaming jungle, a bwana and his faithful native bearer hacking their way through man-eating plants with leaves the size of elephant ears, while the pith-helmeted and netted mistress swoons in the stifling heat. True, most of our plants used indoors do come from warm climates, but what is popularly conceived as jungle exists only in the lowland, equatorial riverbeds of the world. Much of the natural habitat of our houseplants is high in elevation and offers surprisingly cool nights. Plants that are indigenous to this kind of climate will do their best in rooms that feel cool or even downright cold to us. Years ago, unheated or poorly heated glass-enclosed porches made perfect homes for ferns and other plants. Recently I saw two huge Boston ferns through the window of a general store in a tiny village in upstate New York. I stopped to inquire about them and found that they were "Oh . . . maybe thirty years old. All we do is clip 'em a bit when the fronds reach the floor." The fronds were fully eight feet long! The storekeeper further explained that the window fernery received filtered light all year round and that the store stayed pretty cool at all seasons, too, particularly during the winter, when the big potbellied stove was banked down for the night.

Houseplants (in fact, all plants) need nights cooler than the days in order to circulate sugars, which have been manufactured in the leaves during the day, to the roots and other growing parts of the plant. The sugar-manufacturing process requires light and so ceases at night. If the nighttime temperature is high, the plant's respiration rate will increase; and this process will cause loss of growth-producing sugars.

But, to face facts, heated rooms are now the order of the day. Fortunately florists and growers have long recognized this state of affairs and have introduced plants tested for their ability to withstand heat as well as low light and low humidity. The list includes most philodendron, monstera, aglaonema, many bromeliads, davallia ferns, *Dracaena Rothiana*, *D. Massangeana*, *D. Sanderiana*, *D. Warneckii*, *Ficus elastica decora* and *exotica*, several of the palms including howea (kentia) and dwarf chamaedorea, pandanus, peperomia, brassaia (schefflera), and most cacti and other succulents, including sansevieria.

### The New Plant

When a plant is removed from the ideal conditions of the greenhouse and brought into the home, it may appear to suffer from the move. Often some of the leaves turn yellow and drop off, causing alarm and muttered threats of lawsuits against the friendly greenhouse man. Usually the dropping of some leaves is the plant's way of adjusting itself to its new environment. When the roots are able to keep the leaves supplied with moisture, despite the greater rate of moisture evaporation from the leaf surfaces caused by the drier atmosphere of your home, your plant should settle down and begin putting out new growth. Give it a good three weeks to get used to its new home. During this period place the plant so as to avoid drafts and blasts of intermittent hot and cold air. And pay attention to proper watering, too.

### Special Needs

Flowering plants such as gardenias, begonias, cyclamen, primulas, chysanthemums, hydrangeas, and poinsettias will keep much longer, and unfold their buds in a natural way, if you can reduce their nighttime temperature to sixty or even fifty-five degrees.

Saintpaulias (African violets), gloxinias, and other gesneriads will not tolerate temperatures much below sixty-five degrees, day or night. But stuffy, drying heat is resented by all flowering plants and, with drafts and drying out, is the cause of most complaints about their performance.

Foliage plants will stand a somewhat higher temperature range because they don't have to support a showy inflorescence. Some exceptions are podocarpus, fatsia, fatshedera, ligustrum, pittosporum, euonymus, and similar evergreen plants. These prefer a moist-cool, even cold, location and are not happy for long in a warm room. Red cordyline, on the other hand, will develop brown tips if it is kept cold. This browning is also noticeable on the edges of the leaves of *Ficus lyrata* and other large, leathery-leaved tropicals when they are exposed to extreme variations in temperature.

### Temperature Requirements*

 Cool: 40–45 degrees F. at night. 55–60 degrees during the day.

Cyclamen, ivy, spring-flowering bulbs, pittosporum, many ferns, and podocarpus are some of the plants that prefer this temperature range. During cloudy weather the daytime temperature may remain at fifty degrees or so.

 Medium: 50–55 degrees at night. 70 degrees during the day.

Araucaria, beaucarnea, cissus, euphorbia, kentia palm, and many ferns are just a few of the plants that prefer this range. On a cloudy day the temperature may remain at sixty degrees.

* Get acquainted with the temperature symbols used here. They are also used in the plant list in Chapter 2, Plants at a Glance.

 Warm: 62–65 degrees at night. 80–85 degrees during the day.

This is the temperature range most likely to be found in today's homes and apartments. Many plants adapt to this range, including aglaonema, begonias, many palms, crotons, the dracaenas, the philodendrons, and others. Plants in this group that undergo a dormant period should be kept a few degrees cooler during this time, until new growth appears.

## LIGHT

Only in the presence of light will green leaves perform their function of making starch and sugar. Without light this essential process cannot take place and the plant cannot live.

Given this inevitable proposition, it is obvious that your success with plants is going to depend upon your ability to analyze and furnish their light needs.

Light intensity is measured in terms of foot-candles. One foot-candle is the amount of light cast by a candle on a surface one foot away in a completely dark room. Fifteen to twenty foot-candles is equivalent to a fair reading light. This light level is sufficient to maintain some plants, such as aglaonema and aspidistra, but will not allow them to grow appreciably. In order to produce sugars and to grow, a plant must receive a sufficient number of foot-candles over the course of a normal day. If your natural light cannot supply enough to meet the plant's needs, you can add artificial lighting as a supplement to your natural source thus raising the foot-candle reading. Or, as an extension of the available natural light, keep artificial light on after dark, thus lengthening the plant's photo period, or "day." Natural or artificial, it's all light to the plant.

### Natural Light

Windows facing south, and unobstructed by buildings or trees, offer the best light.

At noon, in full sun in the winter, 5,600 foot-candles can be expected at positions ranging from right up against the glass to three feet away. Shaded southern exposures offer nine hundred down to two hundred foot-candles depending on distance from the window.

East and west windows, on a sunny winter's day at noon, offer from 750 foot-candles at the glass to 180 foot-candles three feet away.

North window readings taken on the same day as those above will range from three hundred to seven hundred foot-candles at the glass, to 220–500 foot-candles one foot away, to 150–250 foot-candles two feet away, to 100–180 foot-candles three feet away. If this window, or any of the windows at the other exposures, have a screen, 25–40 percent less light will be admitted. If the exposures are obstructed by outside elements such as buildings or trees, the readings will be reduced 40–50 percent. Positions at the sides of windows will receive less light than positions directly in front of the windows.

Outdoors the light is of course more intense. In the latitude of New York City, a reading of seven thousand foot-candles can be expected on a bright, sunny winter's day at noon. A summer reading from the same spot, taken under the same conditions, should increase by about three thousand foot-candles.

## Artificial Light

Cool, white, fluorescent lights have been used for years as sources of supplementary plant illumination. In recent years special fluorescent and incandescent lights have been developed especially for plants. The Gro-lux line, manufactured by Sylvania, and Plant-gro, manufactured by Westinghouse, are designed to emit high levels of blue and red, the part of the spectrum most utilized by plants. Recently the Duro-lite Company came out with Vitalite, which has been acclaimed by cactus fanciers. Duro-lite also make Optima and Naturescent, which are preferred by bromeliad growers. These special fluorescent

Fluorescent tubing gives off a cool light, so plants can be placed close to it without danger of burning their leaves.

tubes are ideal for use in growing plants in the cellar, in closets, under beds, and in other out-of-the-way places, as well as in low-light areas of the living spaces in the house.

One of the objections I have to some of the fluorescent tubes is that they cast a red to lavender glow over not only the plant but over everything else in the room. And placing furniture and humans in subordinate roles to plant culture is not the way to achieve a harmonious balance in living and in interior decoration. These violet-colored tubes can be used at night when they won't be seen by sleeping people. An automatic timer can turn them on after bedtime and shut them off after the correct number of hours.

Always allow your plants a period of relative darkness so that they can stop their sugar-manufacturing process for a while and send the finished product off to the roots and stems and other growing parts. And don't worry about reversing night and day for your plants; they won't mind a bit.

Fluorescent tubes remain cool while in use, and plants can be placed close to them without danger of burning. For the best decorating effect, however, the tubing should be away from the plants and, if possible, out of sight altogether.

The way to achieve maximum light intensity and flexibility of placement from a fluorescent fixture is to build it yourself. A piece of pine or a strip of plywood can serve as a base to which the components will be attached. All the parts can be purchased at an electrical-supply store. Ask for rapid-start components. If you plan on using the special plant tubes, you might have to look for them at a florist- or plant-supply store. They range in length from twenty-four inches up to ninety-six inches.

**Fluorescent tubing can be hidden behind draperies. Special valances or louvers can be built for permanent disguises.**

Hook up your ballast transformer at some distance (you can go to fifteen feet) from the fixture, because damaging heat tends to build up under the tubing when it is attached. For maximum light intensity, place your tubes two inches apart. The more tubes you use, the more light you get (four 40-watt tubes provide a plant two feet away with 320 foot-candles). Cover the wood base with non-glossy Con-Tact paper in order to reflect all available light outward toward the plant.

Normally, incandescent bulbs give off heat which can burn delicate plant tissues. When the bulbs are placed at a safe distance, their light is often insufficient to maintain proper illumination levels. Recent developments in incandescent lighting for plants have made new types of floodlights available which direct their heat backward, so that the light reaching the plants is cool. General Electric's new Cool-beam spot is valuable for keeping larger houseplants happy without having to surround them with fluorescent fixtures. Plants that will benefit are those that usually don't require bright light, such as the palms, dracaenas, dieffenbachias, and philodendrons.

### Light Requirements*

 Bright light. Full sun: 4,000 to 8,000 foot-candles.

Plants placed in this group should receive the direct rays of the sun over the course of an average day. Bright light is needed by most flowering plants and temperate-zone trees and shrubs. Flowering bulbs should be placed in a bright location until flower buds show color. Plants requiring bright light for maximum growth will tolerate a much lower maintenance level of from five hundred to two thousand foot-candles, if this light is spread over a sixteen-hour photo period, or "day."

* Get acquainted with the light symbols used here. They are also used in the plant list in Chapter 2, Plants at a Glance.

Good light. Filtered or diffused sun: 1,000 to 3,000 foot-candles.

Plants suitable for this location need the kind of light that would be found at a clear, east window in summer. Plants in this group can scorch if placed in the direct rays of the sun, so make sure that south windows are lightly shaded by venetian blinds, bamboo slats, or a filmy curtain. Plants in this group will tolerate a maintenance level of from one hundred to one thousand foot-candles over a sixteen-hour photo period.

 Medium light. No sun: 150 to 500 foot-candles.

Shade-tolerant plants, such as ferns, should be at home in this light. Unobstructed north and east windows, with about half of the sky obstructed by buildings or trees, should yield medium light.

 Low light: 100 to 150 foot-candles.

Plants in this group will maintain themselves in a healthy condition but will put out very little new growth. Areas offering low light, such as obstructed north windows and positions removed from windows, are likely spots for the installation of artificial lighting.

## MOISTURE

Water constitutes 90 percent of a plant's makeup, carries its food supply, and frequently keeps it from collapsing. The plant draws water from the soil through its roots, circulates the moisture throughout its system, and then transpires it into the air through its green parts. How much water is drawn in and then transpired depends upon several factors, including the size of the plant's root system, the availability of moisture in the soil, and the dryness of the air. In the growing area of high humidity, the air will tend to be

waterlogged; and so transpiration of additional water vapor will be inhibited. In this case, less water will be drawn from the soil by the roots. Unless the soil is of a coarse consistency and drains well, the water will remain in the soil and keep air from reaching the root system. Root rot can result.

The idea, then, is to keep a supply of water circulating through the plant— in through the roots, up the stem, and out through the leaves. The speed of this process can be controlled by manipulating the humidity in the air.

### Humidity

Most plants like a relative humidity of around 50 percent. Saintpaulias, orchids, ferns, and others prefer even more—70 percent would not be too much for them (in nature, ferns often grow in areas of 95 percent humidity). As the relative humidity rises, keep good air circulation in order to avoid mildew and fungus.

In today's houses, particularly those heated by steam, the humidity can drop as low as 15 percent in winter. Not only is it difficult for plants to thrive under this condition, but humans don't find it too healthy either. Try to aim for an average relative humidity of 50 percent and lower the temperature to seventy degrees during the day. You and your plants will be happier and healthier.

An automatic humidifier can be a boon to plant and man alike. But even without one there are ways you can add moisture to the air. If you've got radiators, place pans of water on top of them or in the back of them. Bowls of water can be placed among your plants, or you can build a watertight tray big enough to set your pots in and keep that filled with water.

An expensive but durable and handsome tray can be made professionally out of stainless steel. Galvanized steel is cheaper and won't last as long. Or you can make your own tray from inexpensive lumber and builder's plastic. 1. Saw 1 x 6 pine boards (redwood would be even better) in half and nail together to form a frame of the proper dimensions. Add a floor to the frame, cut from marine plywood. 2. Calk all seams and joints with waterproof calking compound, and paint the interior with a waterproof epoxy paint. 3. Line the interior with a continuous sheet of heavy-gauge builder's plastic, stapling the material high up on the inner sides of the tray. Make sure that there are no seams, openings, or tiny tears in the plastic. 4. Spread *smooth* pebbles (sharp stones can rip the plastic) almost to the top, and add water until it reaches just below the top layer of pebbles. Take the greatest possible care in making your pebble tray waterproof. Even the tiniest amount of water seepage will cause an unnoticed wet spot underneath the tray, and floor damage is sure to result.

Frequent misting of the foliage keeps ferns and other plants happy, but can be a chore. Saintpaulias, gloxinias, and other plants with hairy leaves should not be misted. Also take care that you don't

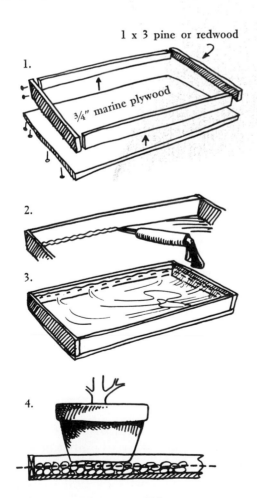

1 x 3 pine or redwood

3/4" marine plywood

**Making an inexpensive pebble tray**

allow water to remain on the crowns of cyclamen, and most other plants too, or they will rot. Good air circulation and ventilation will solve most mildew and rot problems. Don't throw up a window right next to your plants, though. Open a window in an adjoining room instead.

### Watering

There's no hard and fast rule on when to water, but a good test is to rub some of the soil between your fingers. If it powders, the plant needs water. If it holds together, no watering is necessary. To make things easier on yourself, group together plants with similar watering requirements and try to naturalize them by planting them in clusters in large containers. When watering a plant, do it thoroughly, not in dribbles. Some plants will like to be kept moist at all times, while others will prefer to dry out a bit between waterings. But no houseplant should be allowed to stand in water. Soak the pot, if you will, but remove it from the basin when air bubbles stop coming to the surface.

If chlorine is present in your water supply, set aside water to be used for plants for at least twenty-four hours, so that it can aerate. Chlorine is a poison to plants and will inhibit their growth.

Plants that are placed in a bright window will require more frequent waterings than those in darker areas. As light is reduced, reduce the frequency of waterings. Keep a close lookout for signs of wilting in plants growing in the direct rays of the sun. Even plants that like full sun can dry out with surprising speed. Filtering the sunlight is often a good idea.

Subirrigation is a method of watering that can save many steps between the plant and the sink. Run a cotton wick through the pot's drainage hole when the plant is potted. Place the pots in deep saucers filled with wet sand. Bury the end of the wick in the sand. Water will be absorbed into the soil by capillary action as it is needed. Make sure that a good amount of drainage material covers the hole in the pot so that excess water can drain back

**Watering by subirrigation**

into the sand. Several pots can be kept moist at once if a large enough tray is provided to hold the wet sand. Place strips of wood across the top of the tray to support the pots, and let their wicks hang down into the sand.

### Moisture Requirements

 Wet: Quite moist to thoroughly wet.

Never let these plants dry out. Subirrigation is a good watering method. Plants in this group love moisture but dislike "wet feet." Exceptions are aquatics and bog plants.

 Moist: Evenly moist but not wet.

Fibrous-rooted plants fall within this group. These plants have hairlike roots which can rot if kept too wet and burn if allowed to dry out. Subirrigation can be used. Don't allow the soil to become waterlogged and "sour." Keep the soil somewhat drier during resting periods and temperature drops.

 Dry: Soak the soil, then allow to dry out before repeating.

Plants in this group have thick, wiry roots which require good air circulation in order to develop a healthy, white root system. Soak the pot in a tub of water until air bubbles stop coming to the surface. A dry atmosphere will cause more frequent waterings. Feel the soil . . . if it's powdery, it's dry.

## SOIL AND NUTRIENTS

Soil is the medium within which a plant's roots wander in search of food and moisture.

Hopefully your newly purchased plants will be potted in the right soil mixture and will have sufficient room in their pot for new root growth. Unfortunately, things are not always as they should be, and this section will be helpful in seeing that you get your money's worth in your plant purchases. Ask your plant man to repot your purchase if it needs it, particularly if the plant is large and costly. Of course, you can also do the repotting yourself at home.

The soil must not be so compacted and hard that it blocks the seepage of water and air into its depths, or so absorbent that it holds water next to the roots for long periods, or so loose that it allows water to evaporate rapidly, leaving the roots to dry out.

Ideally, potting mixtures should be friable and light so that water and air move quickly through. This condition can be best achieved by mixing just the right proportions of such ingredients as loam, leaf mold, peat moss, various grades of bark, sand, gravel, wood ash, bone meal, perlite or vermiculite, well-rotted cow or sheep manure, and more. Luckily you won't have to stock up on all of these ingredients because the vast majority of houseplants will thrive in several basic mixtures, soil or soilless, that are easy to mix.

### Soil Mixtures

If you want to use your own garden soil, you can combine it in a number of ways with a variety of ingredients. A good basic mixture is equal parts of garden loam, peat moss, and clean, sharp builder's sand.

Make sure that the soil mix is friable, or loose, when moderately wet. Test it by crushing some in your hand. If it falls apart when you open your hand, you've got a good formula. If it remain in a ball, you need more organic matter. Add some horticultural perlite to the mix to keep it light. Bone meal and wood ash are good additions and so is coarse, well-aged cow or sheep manure. Avoid an overrich soil, since undue stimulation can lead to rank and ragged growth.

Most tropical plants prefer a pH value of from 5.5 to 6.5, a moderately acid (as opposed to alkaline) soil condition which is promoted by the addition of leaf mold, humus, or peat moss. You can determine the pH of your soil mixture by sending a sample of it to your county agricultural agent for analysis. Also, do-it-yourself testing kits are available at most garden-supply centers.

Soil mixes should be pasteurized in order to destroy insects, their larvae and eggs, fungus, and weed seeds. Some plants, like saintpaulias, demand a pasteurized soil. Others appreciate it and will respond better to a sterile soil condition. Fill a large baking pan with four inches of well-moistened but not soggy soil mix, and bake in a two-hundred-degree oven for two hours. If you have a meat thermometer, check when the soil temperature reaches 185 degrees and give it another thirty minutes. Small amounts of mix can be sterilized in a pressure cooker. Place a pan of soil on the rack over an inch of water and raise the pressure to fifteen pounds for one hour. Don't use your pasteurized soil for several days after treatment.

## Soilless Mixes

The New York State College of Agriculture at Cornell University has developed two new artificial mixes that are being used increasingly by commercial growers for their tropical plants. The "Cornell mixes" are of value to home plant-growers as well. They can hold moisture and nutrients for beneficial periods, and since they use no loam or natural soil, they are already sterile and require no pasteurization. Plants that grow well in the Cornell Foliage Plant Mix include ferns, palms, geraniums, amaryllis, aphelandra, begonia, beloperone, buxus, caladium, cissus, citrus, coleus, ficus, hedera helix cultivars, helxine, maranta, oxalis, pilea, sansevieria, and tolmiea.

The Cornell Foliage Plant Mix consists of:

| | | |
|---|---|---|
| Sphagnum peat moss (screened through 1½" mesh) | 1 | bushel |
| Number 2 vermiculite | ½ | bushel |
| Medium perlite | ½ | bushel |
| Ground dolomitic limestone | ¾ | pound |
| Superphosphate, 20% powdered | 3 | ounces |
| 10-10-10 fertilizer | 4 | ounces |
| Iron sulfate | 1 | ounce |
| Potassium nitrate | 1½ | ounces |
| Peter's Soluble Trace Element Mix | 1½ | grams |

The second formula, Cornell Epiphytic Mix, is useful for those plants that usually grow on other plants, using them for support. These include bromeliads, episcia, hoya, monstera, nephytis, pothos, syngonium, saintpaulia, aglaonema, aloe, cactus, crassula, dieffenbachia, gloxinia, philodendron, and peperomia. This mix provides good drainage:

| | | |
|---|---|---|
| Douglas fir bark, fine grade | 1 | bushel |
| Medium perlite | 1 | bushel |
| Sphagnum peat moss (screened through ½" mesh) | 1 | bushel |
| Ground dolomitic limestone | 1 | pound |
| Superphosphate, 20% powdered | 10¾ | ounces |
| 10-10-10 fertilizer | 5⅓ | ounces |
| Iron sulfate | 1⅓ | ounces |
| Potassium nitrate | 2 | ounces |
| Peter's Soluble Trace Element Mix | 3½ | grams |

Perlite and vermiculite are volcanic minerals which are expanded by heat into lightweight pebbles filled with air bubbles which attract and hold moisture. These and fir bark, limestone, superphosphate, iron sulfate, potassium nitrate, and the soluble fertilizer and trace element mix should be available at any good-sized garden center. If you've got a commercial grower in your area, perhaps he will help you with some of the ingredients. Remember to combine them thoroughly. Another good thing to keep in mind is that Douglas fir bark must be kept damp at all times. It is very difficult to moisten uniformly again once it dries out.

### Nutrients

Curb your instinct to treat your plants to lavish feasts and follow the directions on the plant-food package. Remember that you can damage your plants by overfertilizing them. Potbound plants require more frequent feeding than those plants having plenty of room to stretch their roots. Recently repotted plants should be fed lightly after a few weeks. If you want to avoid overfeeding, add a quarter *level* teaspoonful of any soluble fertilizer per gallon of water and use this solution every time the plants needs watering.

Fertilizer salts can build up in the soil, particularly if the plant has remained in one pot for many months. At every watering, always add an excess of water so that some flows out of the drainage hole. Then, once a month, flush each pot thoroughly with plain water.

### Pots and Potting

Pots are usually made from two materials, clay and plastic. Each has its good and bad points. Clay pots look better than plastic, drain better, and allow for better air circulation around the roots. They also dry out more quickly than plastic pots, and plants in them will require more frequent watering.

Plastic pots are cheaper, easier to keep clean, and don't allow water to evaporate through the sides. But if the soil isn't light and doesn't drain quickly, an inexperienced gardener can overwater in them.

New and used pots of either material should be scrubbed in a 9 to 1 solution of

**Potting or repotting a plant**

water and Clorox to remove algae and dirt. Soak clay pots in water overnight, to leach out harmful chemicals used in manufacture. Check all pots to make sure that drainage holes are open.

Don't transplant from a pot into too large a new pot. Use only the next size up. Shift plants when their root ball is solid and covered with a network of healthy white roots. Place pieces of broken pottery over the drainage hole to prevent seepage of soil, and sift in a layer of potting mix. The amount of mix under the root ball should be sufficient to elevate it to within a half an inch of the top of the pot. Be sure to allow for settling of new soil when water is added. Firm the soil around the root ball by thumping the pot on the table a couple of times, or by pressing the soil around the roots with your fingers. Place the pot in a pan of water until the surface of the soil is thoroughly wet. Check to make sure that excess water runs quickly through the drainage hole.

## INSECT PESTS AND DISEASES

Sooner or later you are going to discover some bugs chewing or sucking away on your precious plants or some noxious mold creeping along a stem or leaf. Fortunately the kinds of insects you are likely to encounter are small in number, and fungus can be easily controlled.

The best defense against insects and disease is to follow good planting and keeping procedures. Remove and destroy fallen leaves and pull off those that are badly spotted and turning yellow. Wash your plants regularly to remove accumulated dust and soot which can clog the pores; you'll be washing away insects and their eggs at the same time. Water your plants properly and on time. Keep the humidity up and the temperature down . . . bugs thrive in a hot, dry atmosphere. Examine plants regularly and often. Get after bugs as soon as they appear rather than waiting for infestations. If your plants become infested with insects or fungus, remove them to an isolation ward and give them special attention. If they don't respond, discard them.

### Insects

Plants can be injured and weakened in several ways by insects. It is important that you correctly identify the insect so that you can apply the right measure for its control.

*Chewing insects:* These insects eat wood, bark, leaves, stems, fruits, and seeds. They bore holes in stems and leaves. Chewing insects are not often found on houseplants and are not much of a problem. Look for worms and caterpillars. Pick off and destroy or use Sevin if infestation occurs.

*Sucking insects:* These remove sap and cell substances and inject toxins into the plant's system. Look for misshapen or off-color foliage.

*Aphids:* Plant lice ⅛-inch long. Green or black. Soft-bodied. They attack soft, new growth and appear in clusters.

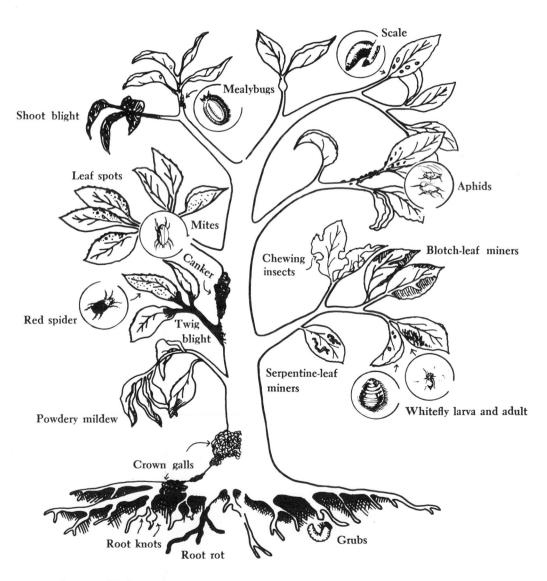

Insect pests you're most likely to encounter

They move about freely and stand on their heads while sucking. They multiply rapidly but can be controlled easily. Look for them on plants growing in a cooler temperature, such as geraniums, fatshedera, ivy, dieffenbachia, ferns, gardenias.

Spray with a nicotine sulfate and soap-flake solution or dip entire plant into this mixture. Wash away insects and their eggs with a forceful jet of water, repeating the treatment every three days. Do this in the bathroom tub or sink and be sure to hit the undersides of the leaves. Alternatives: spray or dip in rotenone and/or pyrethrum formulas. Use a systemic insecticide. Spray or dip in Sevin.

*Mealybugs:* Slow-moving, pinkish-white, soft-bodied, and many-legged. They are covered with a whitish, waxy substance which often resists penetration by insecticides. The young emerge from cottony masses and are easier to kill. Look for mealybugs on the undersides of leaves and in their axils. They are often found on saintpaulias, dieffenbachias, dracaenas, gardenias, ferns, syngonium, cissus, philodendrons, begonias, coleus, fuchsia, gloxinia, and palms.

Spray or dip with nicotine sulfate (Blackleaf 40) and white summer oil. Direct forceful jets of water at massed insects. Apply alcohol or ether with a Q-tip. Spray or dip with rotenone-pyrethrum combined with white summer oil. Spray or dip with white summer oil only (use as directed; oil can damage foliage). Use a systemic insecticide. Use Sevin as a spray or dip.

*Mites:* Microscopic, oval-shaped, and spiderlike. The broad mite moves quickly and feeds on the exposed undersides of the leaves of ivy, fatshedera, cissus, and aralia. The cyclamen mite is more slow-moving and is harder to get at, because it likes to suck on the new, tender growth of saintpaulias, ivy, cissus, begonias, and episcias. The hairy leaves of gesneriads make it especially difficult to reach the mites with insecticide, so take extra care to force the mixture into the areas of the plant where new growth is forming. Also look for mites on geraniums, palms, pittosporum, podocarpus, and brassaia.

Apply the miticide Kelthane. Apply a systemic insecticide such as Cygon.

*Red spider:* These tiny mites can be seen through a magnifying glass. Look for them on the undersides of leaves, where they may spin webs. They reproduce rapidly, laying transparent eggs the size of a pinpoint. Look for speckling and discoloration of the leaf surfaces of ivy, araucaria, aspidistra, maranta, and red cordyline.

Spray or dip with nicotine sulfate and white summer oil. Syringe with forceful jets of water every three days. Spray or dip in rotenone and/or pyrethrum mix. Spray or dip in white-summer-oil solution. Spray or dip in Kelthane solution. Apply a systemic insecticide.

*Scale:* Tan, brown, black, or white turtle-shaped insects. Their hard outer shell is a waxy substance which protects the soft body underneath. The young move around and are easy to kill. Look for the cottony substance which covers them. Scale can be found on palms, ferns, ficus, citrus, ivy, cactus, pandanus, orchids, philodendron, and bromeliads.

Spray or dip in nicotine sulfate and white summer oil solution. Spray or dip with nicotine sulfate and soap-flake solution. Spray or dip in foliar oil spray. Apply a systemic insecticide. Spray or dip in Sevin. A Q-tip or soft brush dipped in insecticide will kill the young. This method is useful in dislodging the hard shells of the adults so that the poison can penetrate to the soft bodies.

*Whitefly:* Immature stages look like pale-green scale insects. Adults look like moths 1/16-inch long, are covered with a white, powdery substance. Look for them on the undersides of leaves, where they suck juices and excrete a honeydew which can clog pores and encourage sooty molds. They attack begonias, citrus, fuchsia, gardenias, geraniums, and other plants.

Spray or dip with rotenone and/or pyrethrum mix. Spray with nicotine sulfate and soap-flake solution. Apply a systemic insecticide. Weekly applications of each of the above may be necessary for control.

## Safe Use of Insecticides

In his efforts to control insect pests, man has developed such potent poisons that he has destroyed not only insects but whole families of wildlife, to say nothing of occasional human beings. At the time of this writing, the government has finally banned certain persistent pesticides for commercial use, yet these same products are still being used as ingredients in insecticides packaged and sold for use in the home. The use of such poisons at home is to be avoided, advertising or point-of-purchase claims to the contrary notwithstanding. The insecticides recommended in this book have been carefully selected for their safety and effectiveness in the home. The use of any "harder" insecticide is like using a shotgun to kill the insect. You get the insect, but you also get the furniture, the plant, the walls, and anyone who happens to be standing within range.

Aerosol dispensers are handy but costly. Their propellant can burn delicate plant tissues.. If you hold the can far enough away from the plant to avoid such damage, the stuff gets all over the house. Dip your plants into a proper solution of the right insecticide, or swab individual insect masses such as scale with a Q-tip or paintbrush dipped into the solution. If you must spray, take the plant outdoors and use a pressure sprayer or hand mister. If the plant is too large to move easily, cover it with a sheet of transparent plastic and spray the insecticide through a small opening.

Store all insecticides and equipment in a cool, dry, well-ventilated cabinet which has a good, strong lock. Never store insecticides in the kitchen. Don't store volatile herbicides, such as 2-4-D or Silvex, near pesticides because the volatile vapors can be absorbed by the pesticide. These products should always be stored in an outside shed or the garage.

Recommended for home use:

*Nicotine sulfate:* Sold under the trade name Blackleaf 40. Use alone as directed. Or mix one teaspoonful with two tablespoonfuls of white summer oil in a gallon of water. A nicotine solution can be made at home by soaking cigar, cigarette, or pipe tobacco in water for a week. Use on mealybugs and scale.

*Nicotine sulfate and soap flakes:* Mix one teaspoonful of nicotine sulfate with two tablespoonfuls of soap flakes in one gallon of water. Useful against aphids, scale, and whitefly.

*Alcohol and ether:* Dip a soft brush or Q-tip in either one and carefully apply to mealybugs and other insects. Whiskey can be used in place of alcohol and nail-polish remover is a good substitute for ether. Apply carefully so that you don't burn tender plant tissue.

*Rotenone and pyrethrum:* These are leguminous sprays and are made from certain plants. Use as directed against aphids, mealybugs, scale, exposed thrips, whitefly, mites, red spider, and other mites.

*Systemics:* These are insecticides which are worked into the soil under the foliage of the plant and are taken in through the roots, becoming part of the sap. Sucking insects are destroyed by the treated sap. One such systemic, Cygon, is mixed one teaspoonful to the gallon of water. It kills aphids, mealybugs, scale, mites, whitefly, thrips, and root mealybugs. Do not use systemics or any other type of insecticide on herbs or other edible plants!

*White summer oil:* A superior grade of petroleum oil which is emulsifiable. Mix from two to three tablespoons to the gallon of water and use with caution no more than once a month. When mixing it with insecticides, use as directed. In this combination, the oil helps penetrate the protective coatings of mealybugs and scale. Caution: do not use oil on gesneriads or other hairy-leaved plants. Apply at a temperature of 70–80 degrees and not in direct sun. Wash off residue in a couple of hours.

*Sevin:* Sold as a wettable powder or in solution. Use as directed against mealybugs, aphids, and other insects.

*Kelthane:* Sold as a wettable powder or in an emulsifiable concentrated form. This miticide is useful and effective against red spider and cyclamen mite. Use as directed.

*Dusting sulfur:* Effective against broad mite. Dust plant in 70–80-degree temperature, and in full sun if possible.

*Syringing:* Forceful syringing with a jet of water will dislodge and wash away many insects and their eggs. Do it every three or four days in the bathtub.

### Fungus and Diseases

Houseplant diseases are a rare problem since they tend to flourish in dampness and the dry atmosphere of most houses discourages their proliferation. Good houseplant-keeping practices will ward off almost any disease.

*Mildew:* Sudden drops or rises in temperature can cause mildew, and so can cold drafts and extended dampness. Karathane is effective and is particularly satisfactory on begonias, kalanchoë, hydrangeas, saintpaulias, and others. Sulfur controls mildew and rust but requires a high temperature in order to vaporize properly.

*Rot:* This term refers to a number of fungus and bacterial conditions. Water each individual plant according to its needs. Avoid "wet feet." Provide good ventilation and soil aeration. Use pasteurized soil in all mixes using garden soil. Apply Bordeaux mixture for leaf spot, anthracnose, rusts, molds, rots, and blights. Use Zineb or Captan against stem rot and leaf spots.

### Fungus and Disease Control

*Karathane:* Sold as a wettable powder. Mix one tablespoonful to two gallons of water and add a soapy spreader to penetrate the waxy powder of mildew.

*Bordeaux mixture:* You can buy this already packaged or you can make your own. Add equal parts of copper sulfate and hydrated lime (one ounce each) to a gallon of water. Use immediately, and as directed for commercial mixes. Effective against fungus and bacterial diseases such as leaf spot, anthracnose, rusts, molds, rots, and blights.

*Zineb:* Sold as a 65% wettable powder. Mix one tablespoonful to each gallon of water. Controls fungus diseases, Botrytis blight, and bacterial leaf spot. The plant may be sprayed or dipped into the solution.

*Captan:* Sold as a 50% wettable powder or as a 7½% dust. Use as directed against fungus diseases and stem rot.

## PROPAGATION

Increasing the numbers of your houseplants by propagation not only saves you money but it's instructive, fun, and easy.

Plants can be reproduced either sexually, from seeds, or asexually, by vegetative means. Seed propagation takes longer but is more practical from a commercial point of view. Vegetative propagation takes advantage of the ability of plants to put out roots from an injured or cut surface. Propagation techniques called "taking cuttings" and "layering" are involved here. Division of various kinds of root systems and the planting of runners and offsets are other easy ways to increase your home nursery.

### Seed

Your soil should be a mixture of equal parts of leaf mold or peat moss, loam, and sand. Pasteurize the mix and also the containers which will be used. A good soilless mix consists of equal parts of peat moss, ground sphagnum moss, and perlite. Sterilize the pots.

Cover the pot's, or other container's, drainage hole with pieces of broken crockery and fill the pot to the brim with your soil or soilless mixture. Tap the pot on the table to settle the soil and sift a fine layer over the top.

**Propagation by seed**

**Propagation by stem and tip cutting**

**Cane cuttings**

Sow seed on the surface of the mixture. Some seed, like begonia, is very fine and shouldn't be covered. Cactus seed likes to be covered with a layer of coarse grit or crushed limestone.

Mist with a fine spray, being careful not to disturb the seeds, and cover the container with a sheet of glass or plastic. Set the pot in a saucer of water until the potting mixture is evenly moist. Repeat as needed.

Maintain a temperature of seventy degrees or above for most seeds. Keep in good light, but out of direct sun, until germination.

When plants develop one or two true leaves, transplant carefully, several seedlings to a pot. When these become crowded, transplant to individual pots.

Seeds from citrus fruits are good bets. Grapefruit, particularly, makes a beautiful glossy-green plant.

Cactus seed is generally very fertile and is easy to germinate. Bromeliad seed can be germinated on four-ply Kleenex tissue, which has been soaked in water. You can germinate other seeds by this method, too.

### Stem Cuttings

The brittle tips, or portions of the stem with eyes, of most plants will root if placed in moist perlite, crushed granite, or sand. Soft cuttings give off more water than they can take in, so cover them with a glass enclosure or a hood of plastic. Fibrous-rooted begonias, scindapsus,

peperomia, and ivy don't need this protection. Hydrangea and gardenia do.

It is important to maintain even moisture in the rooting medium. A clay pot that is kept full of water, plunged into the center of the larger pan holding the cuttings will do the trick.

Take cactus cuttings by cutting the joints with a sharp knife. Dip the wound in charcoal and allow it to dry for a few days. Then plant it shallowly in dry sand until it roots.

Succulents, such as crassula and sedum, can be propagated by tip cuttings.

*Dracaena Warneckii, D. terminalis,* and dieffenbachia canes can be cut and the ends powdered with charcoal. New plants will sprout continuously from hidden eyes, or the entire section of cane can be planted, producing a single plant.

Hardwood cuttings can be taken from crotons, hibiscus, citrus, jasmine, and other heat-loving shrubs. Insert cutting two-thirds of its length in sandy peat moss and keep moist.

Geraniums, wax begonias, fuchsia, impatiens, coleus, aucuba, dracaena, gardenia, saintpaulia, hibiscus, tradescantia, cissus, cyperus, ivy, and philodendron will root in a glass of plain water.

If your philodendron has grown scraggly, cut off a tip with three to five leaves and some aerial roots attached, and pot into a rough mixture of peat moss, loam, sand, and rotted manure. Train against a slab of bark or a moss-covered pole which has been soaked in nutrients.

Pineapples can be propagated by cutting off the bristly tops, scraping away all traces of juicy flesh, and drying them out for ten days prior to planting on sand which is kept moist. After roots have formed, transplant to a potting mix.

Joint cuttings can be taken from some of the philodendrons and from dieffenbachia. Break them from eyes when the temperature is warm and humid. Place them in a tray or pan filled with moist peat moss or sphagnum until roots develop. Then plant in potting mixture.

### Leaf Cuttings

Tropical plants with fleshy leaves and prominent veins can often be propagated by cutting the leaves in various ways and inducing roots to form at the wound.

Peperomia, saintpaulia, many begonias, gloxinias, streptocarpus, and many succulents such as crassula, kalanchoë, sedum, echeveria, and sansevieria can be increased by leaf cuttings. Using a sharp knife or razor blade, remove individual leaves, each with an inch of stem. Plant the leaf, stem end first, in sharp sand, perlite, or crushed stone. Keep the planting medium moist and transplant when roots and new plantlets form. Keep in

**Propagation by leaf cuttings**

good light, but not direct sun. A plastic bag or a pan of glass for a cover increases humidity.

Saintpaulias, gloxinias and other gesneriads, and begonias will sprout leaflets from cuts in their leaves. Remove mature, healthy leaves, keeping an inch of stem, and cut the ribs in several places. The stalk end of the leaf is placed in the rooting medium and the leaf itself is laid flat on the medium and held in place with pegs or pebble weights (the pegs or weights insure that the cuts are held tightly against the medium). Cover with glass or plastic. New plants will grow from the cuts in the parent leaf and should be separated and planted in potting mix as soon as strong roots and well-formed leaves develop.

Rex begonia leaves can be cut into sections which will root and produce new plants. Remove a healthy leaf and make three or four wedge-shaped cuttings from it. Each cutting must have a main vein as well as a slice from the leaf stem. Insert the wedge-shaped cuttings, point down, in sand or perlite with a bit of peat moss mixed in. The leaf base should be at sand level. Water thoroughly and cover with a clear plastic tent. Don't let the cuttings touch each other or the plastic, or rotting will result. Keep the cuttings in good light, but not in direct sun. In three or four weeks, when plantlets appear, transplant entire cutting into potting mix.

### Air Layering

*Ficus lyrata,* dracaena, crotons, coccolobis, ardisia, and other plants can be propagated by causing shoots to put out roots while the shoots are still attached to the parent plant.

With a sharp knife or razor blade, make a clean cut upward into the stem of the shoot which you wish to root. Insert wet sphagnum moss into the cut and pack it around the outside. Cover the bundle of wet moss with plastic film to hold in moisture. As soon as sufficient roots have formed, remove the plastic and moss. Cut the shoot, with its root system, from the parent plant and plant in potting mix.

### Division

Many plants can be split apart at their bases and the root and stem pieces repotted. These include ginger, calathea, cyperus, spathiphyllum, many ferns, older saintpaulias, aspidistras, and cypripedium orchids.

Chrysanthemums, acorus, astilbe, aspidistra, sansevieria, and some ferns produce rhizomes, which are underground stems complete with leafbuds or eyes. Divide and plant.

**Division**

**Bulb and "bulblet"**

Tubers can be divided into as many pieces as they have eyes. Some plants with tubers are caladium, canna, and alocasia.

Amaryllis, clivia, and other plants form bulblets at the end of their bulbs. Remove, after flowering, and plant. Lily bulbs have scales which may be removed and planted.

Cattleya orchids bear pseudo-bulbs which can be cut when the front eye swells and new roots begin to appear. Pot in osmunda fiber or shredded fir bark.

**Propagation by air layering**

155

**Suckers**

Offsets

### Suckers

Staghorn-ferns, most bromeliads, musa, agave, pandanus, and echeveria are some of the plants which produce suckers from their bases. Break or cut from the mother plant and allow to root in potting mix.

### Offsets and Runners

Boston ferns produce long, stringlike runners which can be planted.

Some plants send out tiny scouts in search of soil. These offsets, or complete plants, can be planted immediately in potting mix. Episcia, saxifraga, and chlorophytum are familiar examples.

# 14. Some Plant Families and Their Environments

## BEGONIAS

### Temperature

Begonias are not necessarily tropical, but most are found from Trinidad to Africa and Asia. They will thrive in normal house temperatures of from sixty-five degrees at night (or several degrees warmer) up to seventy-five degrees during the day. The daytime temperature can go on up to eighty degrees, but this is the top of the range. Feel the leaves of your begonias. If the leaf feels warm, the plant isn't happy. The tropical varieties, such as *B. pustulata*, Rex 'Iron Cross', *B. cathayana*, and the rare *B. goegoensis* can take a warmer daytime temperature, but the nighttime drop should not be more than five degrees.

Cold or drastic temperature changes will prove disastrous to the varieties mentioned above, but the more hardy semperflorens begonias will tolerate cool temperatures. On cold nights, place newspaper between the window glass and the plants. Avoid drafts for all begonias.

### Light

In their natural habitat begonias receive filtered sunlight, and this is the condition you should try to duplicate in your home. Where full sun is available, a window facing east is ideal. The plants will benefit from the good light and the cooler morning sun. The semperflorens and cane-stemmed varieties take the greatest amount of sunlight and the Rex begonias the least. Where full sun is expected for most of the day, filter the strong light with sun-loving plants and place your begonias where they will receive partial shade from them.

A north window, away from the sun, is best for Rex begonias. These plants will drop leaves in the fall, a sign of their approaching rest period. When new buds appear in the spring, give them more light by moving them to an east window. Or supplement their light from the northern exposure with artificial lighting.

### Moisture

Rex begonias are tropical and like a high humidity. They should be kept evenly moist at the roots. A good method is to water from a saucer under the pot, by subirrigation. The more hardy semperflorens and cane-stemmed varieties should be allowed to dry out and then should be soaked all the way through. All begonias will suffer from root rot if kept overly wet. Their roots will shrivel and burn if kept too dry.

The pebble-water tray will raise the humidity of the air surrounding your begonias. The tray is especially recommended for use with the sun-loving varieties, which can dry out if not watched closely. Begonias will be happiest in an average humidity of around 50 percent.

### Soil and Nutrients

Begonias prefer a soil mixture which is loose, well drained, slightly acid, and rich in humus or other organic matter. A good general begonia mix consists of two parts garden loam; one part humus, leaf mold, or peat moss; and one part sharp sand. Add a small amount of well-rotted manure, some broken or pulverized charcoal, and a pinch of bone meal or a sprinkling of some other organic fertilizer. For Rex begonias the mix may be lighter, with less loam and more humus. For semperflorens begonias, use less humus and more soil.

For a soilless mix, combine one part peat moss, two parts chopped sphagnum moss, and one part horticultural perlite.

Don't feed your begonias directly after flowering or when the plant is dormant. Hold back food if the plant is weak or leggy or if it has just been repotted. At other times use a good commercial water-soluble fertilizer. Mix it at half the strength recommended on the label and use it twice as often.

### Insect and Fungus Control

Begonias are not prone to insects and disease. A forceful syringing will dislodge most bugs. Infestations of aphids, plant lice, or black fly may be eliminated with nicotine sulfate and soap-flake mix. Mealybugs can be attacked with a cotton swab dipped in alcohol. Red spider and mites can be controlled with rotenone.

Keeping your begonias clean and healthy will help them to ward off most fungus, providing that your watering procedure is correct. Damp weather might bring on a touch of mildew. A light dusting of sulfur or a spray of wettable sulfur will control it.

Sudden defoliation or loss of flower buds or yellowing of leaves can be caused by environmental conditions, not by insects or diseases. Avoid temperature changes, excessively dry air, or sudden shifts from a sunny location to a shady one. Root rot, caused by overwatering, shows up as a yellowing and dropping of leaves. Root burn can be caused by overfertilizing or underwatering and can be evidenced by sudden wilting. Brown leaf tips and brown spots on foliage can be caused by sunburn, dry or hot air, improper watering, or by objects rubbing against the leaves.

### Propagation

The semperflorens, or wax, begonias are most often propagated from seed.

If you want to reproduce a named variety, grow your new plants from cuttings. Base or midstem is best to use for cuttings, as tips often will not branch.

Rex, other rhizomatous, and tuberous-rooted begonias may be propagated by the leaf-cutting method. You can also peg the entire leaf flat against the rooting mixture and make several right-angled cuts through the main veins.

## BROMELIADS

### Temperature

Bromeliads tolerate a wide range of temperature variation, from near freezing to a high room temperature. But since most of them come from tropical or subtropical regions, don't expect them to thrive under cold conditions. Seventy degrees during the day and fifty-five degrees at night is ideal, but the range can be in-

creased safely by five degrees. If the plants are being grown on a windowsill, tape the cracks in order to keep out frigid blasts of winter air. Some air circulation is important and can be safely supplied by leaving a window open in another room.

### Light

Bromeliads will survive under surprisingly low light conditions, but they must have good light in order to reach their full potential in flower and foliage. In non-urban areas, an east, west, or south window should furnish sufficient light. In cities, particularly those with smog conditions, even a southern exposure may admit only a relatively small percentage of usable light. Generally, the guzmanias, vriesias, and nidulariums will tolerate lower light levels. Cryptanthus, neoregelias, and tillandsias require good light; and the aechmeas, ananas (pineapples), billbergias, and dyckias prefer bright light. A helpful rule of thumb to remember is that the softer and more pliable the leaf, the less light is required; and the stiffer and harder or more spined or more heavily scaled the leaf, the more light is needed.

Fluorescent fixtures can be kept on for fifteen to sixteen hours a day. Since bromeliads will take the brightest light available, you may increase the light intensity of commercial fixtures by adding tubes or by making your own fixtures. A minimum of four parallel tubes is recommended. Those bromeliads requiring the most light should be placed not farther away than twenty-four inches from the tube. It follows that the guzmanias, vriesias, and nidulariums will be content to occupy the positions farthest away from the tubes.

### Moisture

Most bromeliads grow attached to trees, and their roots are adapted to support the plant rather than to take in moisture. These epiphytic bromeliads grow in regions where they receive a heavy bath of dew at night and where constant rainfall keeps their cups full of water. You should try to duplicate these conditions. A cold-mist humidifier or the water-and-pebble tray will help. If their cups are filled with water, you can safely leave your bromeliads for two or three weeks.

### Soil and Nutrients

Almost any light and porous material rich in humus will serve. Quick drainage of water and air circulation around the roots is essential, so let peat moss, leaf mold, or fir bark make up a third of the mix. Then add perlite or gravel, alone or in combination, some broken pots, sand, charcoal, and some organic fertilizer. Chopped orchid bark (osmunda) and shredded tree fern are good additions to the mixture if you can find them. For terrestrials such as cryptanthus and ananas, add a small amount of potting soil. The Cornell Epiphytic Mix is perfect for bromeliads. Look for the formula in the section on soil and nutrients in Chapter 13, Plant Care.

Occasional mild feeding at monthly intervals with some organic or water-soluble complete synthetic plant food will result in strong growth. Chemical fertilizer should be used more diluted than the package recommends. Spray or pour it directly onto the leaves, and they will utilize it directly.

You can initiate premature flowering, before normal blooming time, practically at will by pouring a solution of calcium carbide (eight to ten pea-sized pellets, five grams or approximately a quarter ounce, dissolved in one quart of water) directly into the funnel at the center of the plant. Flowering should begin, provided that the plant is sufficiently mature, within four weeks for billbergias, six weeks for many aechmeas, and eight weeks for vriesias.

A more organic way to induce flowering is to drain all the water from the cup of a healthy, mature plant and then to place it in an airtight plastic bag together with a big, ripe, fragrant apple. After four or five days the plant is removed, its funnel filled with water, and the apple is eaten. From six to fourteen weeks later, depending on the genus involved, the bromeliad will start to show its inflorescence.

If you wish to grow your bromeliads epiphytically, on a driftwood log or "bark" tree, bore holes in the wood large enough to receive the roots of the plant after they've been wrapped in moistened sphagnum moss. Tie the plant securely in place. Keep the humidity up or mist twice daily with an atomizer. And don't ever let those cups dry out!

### Insect and Fungus Control

Bromeliads are almost entirely pest-free. Soft brown or hard black scale may develop, but you can usually remove them by sponging with a solution of scale oil and a forceful syringing with a jet of water. If the scale refuses to become dislodged, scrape them and repeat the process.

### Propagation

Suckers, or offshoots, can be cut off when they are big enough to handle and rooted in moist sphagnum moss. Raising bromeliads from seed is tricky and time-consuming.

## CACTI

### Temperature

The active growing season for most cacti begins in the spring, when they should get as much fresh air as possible. Set them on a windowsill or even out of doors. As the days become hotter, keep the air circulating. Cool nights are beneficial to cacti.

Near the beginning of winter move your cacti to a cool place (forty-five to fifty degrees) for a resting period. Desert cacti, and those from the high Andes, should actually be chilled. Keep them nearly dry and water them no more than once a week, and only on sunny days. Lobivia and rebutia, especially, must be kept bone-dry and near freezing in an airy spot in order to bloom.

Christmas cacti are true members of the cactus family, although they are na-

tive to tropical mountains and forests rather than to the desert. They like a cooler temperature (sixty to sixty-five degrees) during their growing season.

### Light

Cacti like bright light during their growing season. In the winter they are at rest and can be stored in a cool, dim attic or basement. Plants so stored will need extra protection in the spring when they are once again exposed to the sun.

Christmas cacti should be rested until early fall, when flower buds begin to form. The failing autumn light triggers bud formation, so you should leave your plants outside for as long as the temperature remains above forty degrees and there is no danger of a heavy rain. When you bring the plant indoors, around the end of October, place it in a sunny and cool window away from artificial illumination. A ninety-second exposure to the beam of a flashlight can hold back bloom for two weeks. Even striking a match near the plant can delay flowering for two days!

### Moisture

In tropical zones, where cold weather does not interrupt plant growth, it is the arrival of the dry season which causes plants to stop their growth and to begin a resting period. Gradually hold back watering at this time and move the plants to a cooler place. As mentioned earlier, desert cacti and those from the high Andes should be watered no more than once a week (once every two weeks would be better). Keep lobivia and rebutia bone-dry. A rebutia not watered at all from October until January should develop buds by the end of this period.

### Soil and Nutrients

In nature, cacti don't grow in pure sand or in areas without vegetation. They prefer to grow among desert scrub where their roots will benefit from decaying organic matter and leaf mold as well as from minerals. The soil of arid regions where cacti are usually found is high in minerals, foods, and lime. These ingredients should be included in the potting soil for your cacti.

*Schlumbergera Bridgesii*, the popular Christmas cactus, the orchid-cactus, and others, are tropical cacti and grow epiphytically, on the branches of trees, in much the same way as the bromeliads. These cacti require a rich but porous soil consisting of one part loam, two parts leaf mold, one part rotted manure, and one part coarse gravel. The Cornell Epiphytic Mix is a good soilless formula. Plentiful feeding will insure bountiful flowering, provided that the plants have been given good light and have been kept cool and dry for a dormant period in the winter.

Soil for other cacti should be porous for good drainage and should fall apart easily. Combine a third of builder's sand (don't use beach sand, it's too saline), a third of good garden loam, and some decayed leaf mold or humus. You may give your older plants a bit of well-rotted manure. Perlite, chopped pumice, or chipped lava may be used in the mix, too. But remember to add plant food during the growing season because these materials are non-nutritious. If you are growing any of the white-hairy cacti, add a pinch of lime to their soil.

Repot cacti in a pot a little larger than the diameter of the plant.

## Insect and Fungus Control

Occasionally mealybugs can be found on cacti. Rotenone, sprayed under high pressure, will penetrate their hiding places. Scale can be controlled by nicotine sulfate and soap flakes if the hard outer shell of the old scale is lifted with a knife or toothbrush so that the mixture can reach the soft bodies underneath. Don't use dormant oil sprays, although these are effective against scale, because they tend to discolor and scar the plant body.

Red spider and thrips can be controlled by spraying with Endrin on three alternate days.

## Propagation

Cactus seed is very fertile and is easy to make germinate. Sterilize your cactus potting mixture and also the container. Sow seed on the surface of the soil and sprinkle on a coarse layer of crushed limestone or grit. Keep the temperature from seventy to ninety degrees and insure constant moisture by watering by subirrigation. Transplant often so that the seedlings have room to stretch out.

Use a sharp knife to make cuttings. Dip the wound in powdered charcoal and allow it to dry for a few days. Then place shallowly in dry sand. When roots form, pot in soil mix or Cornell mix.

## FERNS

### Temperature

Ferns that are suitable for indoor growing are mostly tropical and subtropical varieties. Their need for high humidity is closely linked to their temperature requirements, and they will suffer if exposed to dry, hot air. Years ago ferns were placed in partially heated rooms or unheated porches, and they thrived. The reason seems to be that transpiration and evaporation are reduced in a cool room, so ferns do not dry out as quickly. And insect pests don't proliferate as much in a cool room. A temperature of seventy-five degrees is too high for ferns. Seventy is better, and a nighttime drop of at least five degrees is necessary for good growth.

### Light

Ferns are suitable for north, east, and west windows, as well as for locations removed some distance from south windows. Although ferns tolerate low light, they will be sure to benefit from as much good light as is possible. Several hours of direct sun will be tolerated, but be sure to filter summer sun.

### Moisture

Ferns are happiest when surrounded by moisture-laden air. In fact, humidity is the most important factor in their culture. Ferns have evolved in an environment in which the relative humidity often exceeds 50 percent, and your job is to try to duplicate this level. Placing their pots on water-and-pebble trays will certainly help. So will mistings and syringings. Group your ferns closely so that their transpiration process is mutually beneficial. A humidifier not only adds moisture to the air but keeps the temperature down and prevents the air from absorbing additional mosture, thus retarding evaporation off the leaves of the ferns.

Ferns shouldn't be overwatered and it is important that the water drains quickly through the growing mixture, leaving it moist but not wet. Check each of your plants daily and water according to the condition of that day. An occasional dunk in the bathtub will refresh your ferns and will help to dislodge insect pests.

### Soil and Nutrients

Most terrestrial ferns prefer a porous, woodsy soil which will retain moisture. Combine a third of friable loam, a third of peat moss or leaf mold, and a third of some coarse drainage material such as sharp builder's sand, sponge rock, or shredded fir bark. Add a very little amount of well-rotted, old cow manure. The epiphytic ferns do best in an even coarser, more fibrous, and porous mixture. Combine coarse peat moss or leaf mold and shredded fir bark or sphagnum moss with some sand and chunks of old cow manure or osmunda fiber.

If your ferns are in active growth and their environmental conditions are satisfactory, fertilizer can make the difference between a vibrant green and a pale color and can add good, healthy growth. Use a high-nitrogen solution once a month starting in late January, and continue through late September.

### Insect and Fungus Control

Mealybugs and scale insects can present a problem to ferns. Beware of commercial spray preparations and plant bombs. They can damage some fern foliage. The best way to get rid of these and other pests is to wash them off with a forceful spray of tepid water. Mealybugs can be removed with a cotton swab.

### Propagation

If your ferns form several crowns, as does the nephrolepis, these can be propagated by division. Ferns with creeping rhizomes, like the davallias, may have their points cut and rooted. Staghorn-ferns grow suckers which can be rooted. Some ferns mother tiny plantlets on their fronds which will root when the fronds are hooked down onto sandy leaf mold. Certain tree-ferns, such as the Hawaiian cibotium and *Alsophila australis*, can be propagated by cutting their tops to any length desired and rooting the cutting in either moist, porous soil or in a container with gravel in shallow water.

## GERANIUMS

### Temperature

Geraniums are tolerant of indoor conditions but will do best if kept fairly cool. A temperature of from fifty to sixty degrees is perfect for most, and the scented varieties like it even cooler by five or so degrees. Good air circulation can help compensate for higher temperatures and will discourage black rot and other troubles.

### Light

All of the geraniums like sun. Some of the zonale types need full sun in order to bloom, and often the rays of the winter sun are not strong enough to bring them to flower. However, many cultivars are available today which have been developed as excellent winter bloomers.

Scented and ivy geraniums require less sunlight than the free-flowering types. All of your geraniums will benefit from some light shade during the summer months, especially if you live in a particularly hot region.

### Moisture

There are two schools of thought on the amount of water you should give to geraniums. One says never let them become too dry and the other says to let them dry out between waterings. Somewhere in the middle is the best path to follow, but you should grow them somewhat on the dry side.

A few varieties of geraniums have thick, succulent stems and lose their leaves during their dormant period. They should be kept dry during this time. Others, such as the scented, ivy, and Martha Washington geraniums need somewhat more moisture than the freely flowering ones.

### Soil and Nutrients

Geraniums are not fussy. Any good garden soil will grow a good plant, but for great results combine three parts garden loam, one part rotted manure, a small amount of any balanced fertilizer, and one-half part of sharp sand. If you are growing your geraniums in a particularly hot window, full of bright sun, make half of the mix peat moss, in order to prevent excessive drying out.

Feed your plants sparingly during the winter months. From March to October, monthly feeding with one-half strength of a water-soluble balanced fertilizer is a good idea. Add food only when plants are potbound and fully grown. Too much fertilizer will cause leggy growth and fewer blooms. Keep plants in their pots even when potbound. Repot them to the next-larger-size pot only when roots have completely filled the old pot.

### Insect and Fungus Control

Aphids are the bane of geraniums, particularly the scented, ivy, and Martha Washington varieties. Control aphids with a nicotine-and-soap-flake solution and a forceful syringing with a jet of water every three days. If aphids persist, use rotenone or pyrethrum preparations.

An old-fashioned bath with a Lysol or a Fels-Naptha solution should control mites and whitefly.

Mealybugs can be washed off with a jet of water or can be attacked with a cotton swab dipped in alcohol.

Overwatering encourages a fungus disease called black rot. This is often observed spreading from the base of the stems or from cut or broken leaf ends. Avoid it by keeping your plants on the dry side and giving them good air circulation.

Yellowing or yellow spotting of the leaves can be caused by overwatering, extreme drying out, gas fumes, starvation, extreme variations in temperature, or virus. Yellow-blotched new foliage indicates a virus that is most often present in winter.

### Propagation

Geraniums can be easily increased by cuttings. Often, if the temperature is warm enough, you can get a stem to root in a glass of water.

Store geraniums over the winter, after digging them from the garden before frost, by shaking the soil from their roots and hanging them upside down in a cool, dry place such as the garage or basement. Cut them down to living tissue and repot them in the spring. You can hold potted geraniums in a semidormant state by storing them in a cool, dark place and by keeping them dry. Gradual reintroduction to water and light will start new growth.

## GESNERIADS

### Light

Most gesneriads require at least a few hours of sunlight, or its equivalent, each day, but too much sun will require filtering. An east or west window is the best exposure for most of the year. During the winter change their location to a southern exposure. If your plants are leggy and spindly, they are not getting enough light. If they are scorched and yellow and hug the pot, they're getting too much. Like all plants, gesneriads lean toward the light, so rotate their pots regularly to keep them well balanced.

Fluorescent lights will allow you to grow gesneriads anywhere. Ready-made plant stands are available in a variety of sizes. These tend to be rather unattractive affairs and are not suitable for terrific decorating effects.

### Moisture

During active growth periods, keep the soil moist. Clean the foliage frequently with room-temperature water. Don't let the temperature of the water vary more than ten degrees from that of the room, or harmful spotting can occur. Bathe gesneriads, especially those with hairy leaves, in a warm shaded place and return them to sunlight after the leaves have dried.

Try to keep humidity within the 40–60-percent range. Grouping plants raises the humidity about their leaves. Place pots on saucers filled with moist sand, or build a water-pebble tray for them.

### Temperature

If you are happy with the temperature of your rooms, chances are that your saintpaulias, gloxinias, columneas, episcias, and other gesneriads will be, too. The range should be from sixty degrees at night to eighty during the day. Don't let gesneriads touch a cold windowpane. Move them back at night or insulate them with sheets of newspaper.

### Soil and Nutrients

Gesneriads prefer a loose and well-drained soil. The addition of leaf mold, compost, or humus promotes luxurious growth. Combine equal parts of peat moss, well-rotted leaf mold, and good garden loam. Add enough sand so that the mixture falls apart after being squeezed in the hand. Pasteurize the mix. If you use the soilless Cornell mix and decide to add some sand, be sure to pasteurize the sand.

Newly purchased plants may seem too large for their containers. After they have spent a few days in their new environment, gently remove them from their pot and examine the root system. Repot in the next-larger-size pot, if they are potbound.

Too much fertilizer can damage gesneriads. Play it safe and add a one-quarter *level* teaspoonful of any soluble fertilizer per gallon of water and use this solution every time you water your plants. Any fertilizer sold for African violets is fine for other gesneriads. To avoid fertilizer salt buildup in the soil, flush out each pot once a month by pouring a quart of fresh warm water slowly through the soil.

### Insect and Fungus Control

The most serious gesneriad pest is the cyclamen mite. It can only be seen through a magnifying glass, so the first evidence of its presence will be distorted and oddly twisted stems and flower blossoms. The mites are usually found on saintpaulias but can travel to other plants if their host is in contact with them. Therefore, isolate infected plants and treat them with repeated applications of Kelthane, used according to directions. Rotenone is also a proven control.

Root nematodes are indicated by unhealthy flowering and growth and by stubby roots or by knots or lumps on the roots. Treat with commercial materials especially formulated for nematode control.

Mealybugs, aphids, spider mites, and whitefly can attack gesneriads. Their control is given in Chapter 13, Plant Care.

Crown rot is a fungus disease which is indicated by the sudden wilting of a plant. Overwatering or a too-heavy soil can cause this condition, especially during cold, dark weather. Prevent its spread by allowing the soil to dry out and by burning the infected plant.

Powdery mildew on the flower stems and leaves causes stunting of the blossoms. Dust lightly with powdered sulfur.

Bud blast or bud drop is the sudden drying, browning, or dropping off the buds of apparently healthy plants. Gesneriads are very susceptible to man-made gas or oil fumes and may refuse to bloom in houses where these fuels are used. Fumes can also contribute to the dropping of buds of new plants just brought home. Low humidity accompanied by high temperatures and insufficient water can work together or separately to cause bud blast. Overfertilization as buds are developing can upset the plant's chemical balance and cause it to drop its buds. Air pollution, insect infestation, and sudden changes in environment are other causes. Check for the existence of any of these conditions and correct them.

### Propagation

Saintpaulias and many other gesneriads can be easily increased from leaf cuttings. Stem cutting is the best method for propagating fibrous-rooted gesneriads such as columnea and aeschynanthus. Achimenes and others with rhizomes can be increased by breaking the rhizomes apart and placing the pieces in a rooting medium. All gesneriads can be increased from seed.

## ORCHIDS

### Temperature

The orchid family sends representatives as far north as the Arctic, but nearly all of the varieties dwell in the tropics or the subtropics. Tropical Asia, including Malaysia and the Philippines, has the greatest number of varieties. Tropical America and Africa come next, with Australia having the least. Temperate North America, Europe, and Northeast Asia are the homes of many orchids which grow terrestrially. Tropical varieties grow epiphytically and usually have the largest and most lavishly colored flowers.

Many orchids can be grown in the house, although they all prefer the controlled conditions of the greenhouse. Commercial growers and orchid specialists are able to provide several ranges of temperature: warm—sixty-two to eighty degrees; intermediate—fifty-five to seventy; and cool—forty-five to fifty-eight degrees. Dendrobium, phalaenopsis, and vanda like it warm and humid. The intermediate temperature range will accommodate cattleya, paphiopedilum, oncidium, and cycnoches. These will be at home in a room where the nighttime temperature is kept at around sixty degrees, and the daytime high doesn't exceed seventy-five degrees. They also like sun. Cool temperatures are for cymbidium, green-leaf paphiopedilum, and odontoglossum. These will do nicely in a glassed-in sun porch or in the east window of a cool room. Odontoglossum has proved itself tolerant of air conditioning provided that the humidity is kept high.

Many orchids may be taken outdoors during the summer months and hung under a tree or arbor. Here cool nights, good air circulation, morning dew, and occasional showers do wonders. Bring your orchids back indoors in the autumn and look forward to renewed vigor in growth and flowering.

### Light

Sunlight is important to most orchids if they are to flower. Species with hard, water-storing pseudo-bulbs will want the most, although they may scorch if the sun is too strong. The kinds with softer growth will want a location, such as an east window in the summer, where they will be protected from the direct rays of the sun. During the winter months, orchids need all the light they can get. An east or south window is preferable.

One thousand to two thousand foot-candles is a good average light intensity for assorted orchids. The reading can be higher if the light is from one side only, as at a window. Cattleyas prefer two to three thousand foot-candles, as long as other environmental conditions are correct. To grow orchids under artificial light, 650 foot-candles have proven sufficient if the light period is extended to sixteen hours.

### Moisture

Orchids like a high humidity, preferably near 70 percent. A pebble-and-water tray will help to achieve this goal.

When plants are in full growth, water them generously. Soak the pot in a bucket of tepid water and wait for the air bubbles to stop coming up.

Epiphytic orchids—cattleya, epidendrum, oncidium, and odontoglossum—like to get slightly dry between waterings providing that the humidity is kept up. A good watering may be needed every three days in summer, while it might take the pots ten days or so to become dry in the winter.

Fir bark shouldn't be allowed to become completely dry because it is difficult to get it evenly moist again. Orchids planted in this material can be left standing in a saucer of water, after a good soaking, until all of the water disappears up into the bark. Don't water until three days after all the standing water has been absorbed.

Vandaceous orchids and phalaenopsis don't have water-storing pseudobulbs and need more than the cattleyas. Paphiopedilums need an even moisture at their roots when grown as terrestrials. Cymbidiums want plenty of water but also require good aeration and drainage.

Clean the leaves of your orchids regularly with soapy water to remove accumulated soot and to keep the pores open.

### Soil and Nutrients

The fibrous roots of the osmunda fern have long been used as the standard potting medium for most epiphytic orchids, especially cattleyas. But other materials give good results, especially shredded fir bark, which is easy to use and is readily available in most parts of the country. A coarse grade affords good drainage for vandas. Medium coarse (¼–⅝-inch particles) is recommended for oncidium,

dendrobium, and epidendrum. Add a little peat moss or perlite for better retention of moisture and food. For paphiopediums, use a finely screened grade of fir bark, or add 20 percent peat moss to the medium grade, to hold moisture. A mixture of 75 percent medium fir bark and 25 percent peat moss is best for phalaenopsis, miltonia, odontoglossum, and lycaste. Cymbidium, peristeria, and phaius like a compost such as two-thirds coarse humus and one-third soil; or one-third fir bark, one-third redwood fiber, and one-third peat moss, plus 15 percent coarse sand.

While orchids growing in osmunda require very little feeding, plants growing in fir bark should be fed regularly since fir bark is especially deficient in nitrogen. Water-soluble ammonium nitrate is a dependable source of nitrogen when given at the rate of one teaspoonful per gallon of water every second or third watering. However, ammonium nitrate has been found to break down fir bark rapidly. A complete fertilizer formula of 30-10-10, diluted one teaspoonful to one gallon of water, has been found satisfactory if given every third watering during periods of active growth and high light intensity. In winter, reduce to half or even one-quarter strength. Water-soluble fish fertilizer can be used, adding one teaspoonful to a gallon of water once every two or three weeks.

### Insects and Fungus Control

Orchids are not especially susceptible to insect infestation or disease provided that nearby plants don't harbor pests and that good air circulation is always available.

Occasionally scale can become entrenched under the bracts covering the pseudo-bulbs of epiphytic plants. Remove these bracts entirely (their protection job is done once the young shoots mature), and treat for scale or whatever other bug is hiding in there.

Too much wetness, poor drainage, and not enough air circulation can foster leaf spot, anthracnose, gray mold, and rot. Leaf spot is confined to the foliage.

Anthracnose hits leaves and stems with dark-brown to black lesions. For both diseases, reverse the faulty environmental conditions, remove infected foliage, and spray with Bordeaux mixture. Gray mold shows up on flowers. Remove those afflicted and be careful of watering procedures. Also lower the humidity. Rot occurs at the base of pseudo-bulbs. Cut out the rotted portion, increase air circulation, and provide better drainage.

## Propagation

Commercial growers propagate orchids by seed but this is a slow, exacting job. You can divide the rhizomes of cattleyas and other genera with pseudo-bulbs. Orchids which form more than one growth at the bottom can also be divided. Dendrobiums form plantlets near the apex of their pseudo-bulbs, which can be removed and planted.

# Appendix

## GLOSSARY OF COMMON NAMES AND BOTANICAL NAMES

*(Note: For tall, medium-sized, and small plants listed alphabetically
by their botanical names, see Plants at a Glance, page 22.)*

Adam's needle   *Yucca filamentosa*
African evergreen   *Syngonium podophyllum*
African fern-pine   *Podocarpus gracilior*
African pine   *Podocarpus*
African tree-grape   *Cissus Bainesii*
African violet   *Saintpaulia*
Air-pine   *Aechmea* (bromeliads)
Airplane-plant   *Crassula cultrata*
Air-plant   *Kalanchoë pinnata*
Air-tree   *Clusia*
Alabaster-plant   *Echeveria*
Almond-geranium   *Pelargonium quercifolium*
Alpine-violet   *Cyclamen*
Aluminum-plant   *Pilea cadierei*
American maidenhair   *Adiantum pedatum*
American rubber-plant   *Peperomia obtusifolia
     variegata*
Angel's-tears   *Helxine*
Angel-wing cactus   *Opuntia microdasys albata*
Angel-wings   *Caladium*
Angora bunny-ears   *Opuntia microdasys albata*
Antelope-ears   *Platycerium*
Apple-cactus   *Cereus peruvianus*
Apple-geranium   *Pelargonium odoratissimum*
Apricot-geranium   *Pelargonium scabrum*
Aralia, false   *Dizygotheca elegantissima*
Aralia-ivy   *Fatshedera*
Areca-palm   *Chrysalidocarpus lutescens*
Argyritis   *Caladium Humboldtii*
Aristocrat-plant   *Haworthia Chalwinii*
Arrowhead   *Syngonium* 'Emerald Gem'
Arrowhead-plant   *Syngonium*
Arrowhead-vine   *Syngonium*
Arrowroot   *Maranta*
Artillery-plant   *Pilea microphylla*
Asparagus-fern   *Asparagus plumosus*
Aurora-borealis plant   *Kalanchoë Fedtschenkoi*
Australian brake   *Pteris tremula*
Australian gum   *Eucalyptus*
Australian ivy-palm   *Brassaia*
Australian laurel   *Pittosporum Tobira*

Australian maidenhair   *Adiantum hispidulum*
Australian nut-palm   *Cycas media*
Australian pine   *Araucaria excelsa*
Australian umbrella-tree   *Brassaia*
Autograph-tree   *Clusia rosea*
Baby-jade   *Crassula argentea*
Baby rubber-plant   *Peperomia obtusifolia*
Baby's-tears   *Helxine Soleirolii*
Bald-old-man   *Cephalocereus polylophus*
Balfour aralia   *Polyscias Balfouriana*
Ball-cactus   *Notocactus*
Ball-fern   *Davallia bullata*
Ball-moss   *Tillandsia recurvata*
Bamboo-palm   *Chamaedorea erumpens,
     Rhapis excelsa*
Barroom-plant   *Aspidistra*
Basket-plant   *Aeschynanthus*
Bead-vine   *Crassula rupestris*
Bear's-paw fern   *Polypodium Meyenianum*
Begonia-cissus   *Cissus discolor*
Begonia tree-vine   *Cissus discolor*
Belgian evergreen   *Dracaena Sanderiana*
Bermuda maidenhair   *Adiantum bellum*
Bird-of-paradise flower   *Strelitzia Reginae*
Bird's-nest cactus   *Mammillaria campotricha*
Bird's-nest fern   *Asplenium Nidus*
Blonde tree-fern   *Cibotium chamissoi*
Bog-rosemary   *Aeschynanthus*
Boston fern   *Nephrolepis exaltata bostoniensis*
Bottle-palm   *Beaucarnea*
Bowstring-hemp   *Sansevieria*
Bowtie-plant   *Gasteria hybrida*
Boxing-glove   *Opuntia mamillata*
Brake-fern   *Pteris serrulata*
Brazilian coleus   *Plectranthus oertendahlii*
Brazilian gloxinia   *Sinningia speciosa*
Breadfruit, Mexican   *Monstera deliciosa*
Breadfruit-vine   *Philodendron pertusum*
Bread-palm   *Cycas*
Bride's-bouquet fern   *Asparagus plumosus*
Broadleaf-podocarpus   *Podocarpus Nagi*

Broad-leaved India rubber   *Ficus elastica decora*
Bromeliad   *Aechmea* and other "vase" plants
Bunch-moss   *Tillandsia recurvata*
Bunny-ears   *Opuntia microdasys*
Burmese fishtail-palm   *Caryota mitis*
Burro-tail   *Sedum morganianum*
Buttons-on-a-string   *Crassula rupestris*
Calamondin   *Citrus mitis*
Calamus-root   *Acorus*
Candelabra-aloe   *Aloe arborescens*
Candelabra-cactus   *Euphorbia lactea*
Candelabra-plant   *Aloe arborescens*
Candle-plant   *Plectranthus oertendahlii*
Cane-palm   *Calamus, Chrysalidocarpus lutescens*
Cape-myrtle   *Myrsine africana*
Caricature-plant   *Graptophyllum hortense*
Carpet-plant   *Episcia*
Carrot-fern   *Davallia*
Cast-iron plant   *Aspidistra elatior (lurida)*
Cat's-claw   *Dracaena*
Cauliflower-ears   *Crassula argentea*
Century-plant   *Agave americana*
Ceriman   *Monstera deliciosa*
Chain-cactus   *Rhipsalis paradoxa*
Chandelier-plant   *Kalanchoë tubiflora*
Cheese-plant   *Philodendron pertusum*
Chenille-plant   *Echeveria leucotricha, E. pulvinata*
Chinese jade   *Crassula arborescens*
Chinese privet   *Ligustrum lucidum (L. texanum)*
Chinese rubber-plant   *Crassula argentea*
Christ plant   *Euphorbia splendens*
Christ thorn   *Euphorbia splendens*
Christmas palm   *Veitchia Merrillii*
Christmas star   *Euphorbia (Poinsettia) pulcherrima*
Christmas-tree plant   *Araucaria excelsa*
Cinderella slippers   *Sinningia regina*
Cinnamon-cactus   *Opuntia rufida*
Claw-cactus   *Zygocactus*
Climbing-beauty   *Aeschynanthus pulcher*
Climbing-begonia   *Cissus discolor*
Coinleaf-peperomia   *Peperomia polybotrya*
Column-of-pearls   *Haworthia Chalwinii*

Coral-aloe   *Aloe striata*
Coral-berry   *Aechmea fulgens, Ardisia crispa*
Coral-cactus   *Rhipsalis cereuscula*
Corazon de Jesus   *Caladium bicolor*
Cordatum-philodendron   *Philodendron oxycardium*
Corkscrew   *Euphorbia mammillaris*
Corncob-cactus   *Euphorbia submammillaris*
Corn-plant   *Dracaena Massangeana*
Cornstalk-plant   *Dracaena Massangeana*
Corsican carpet-plant   *Helxine Soleirolii*
Corsican curse   *Helxine Soleirolii*
Cotton-pole cactus   *Opuntia vestita*
Cow-tongue cactus   *Gasteria*
Crab-cactus   *Schlumbergera, Zygocactus truncatus*
Crane's-bill   *Geranium*
Creeping-Charley   *Pilea nummulariaefolia*
Cretan brake   *Pteris cretica*
Crimson-cup   *Neoregelia farinosa*
Crocodile-jaws   *Aloe humilis*
Crown-of-thorns   *Euphorbia splendens*
Curiosity-plant   *Cereus peruvianus monstrosus*
Curly-palm   *Kentia (Howea) Belmoreana*
Curtain-plant   *Kalanchoë pinnata*
Cushion-aloe   *Haworthia*
Cut-leaf   *Philodendron pertusum*
Cutleaf-philodendron   *Monstera deliciosa*
Dagger-fern   *Polystichum acrostichoides*
Date-palm   *Phoenix dactylifera*
Deer's-foot-fern   *Davallia canariensis*
Delta-maidenhair   *Adiantum cuneatum*
Devil's-ivy   *Scindapsus (Pothos)*
Devil's-tongue   *Sansevieria*
Devil's-walking-stick   *Aralia spinosa*
Dish-fern   *Pteris*
Dollar-plant   *Crassula argentea*
"Dracaena"   *Cordyline*
Dracaena-palm   *Dracaena indivisa*
Dragon-bones   *Euphorbia lactea*
Dragon-tree   *Dracaena Draco*
Drop-tongue   *Schismatoglottis*
Duff's sword-fern   *Nephrolepis Duffii*
Dumb-cane   *Dieffenbachia*
Dumb-plant   *Dieffenbachia*
Dusty-miller   *Centaurea candidissima, C. gymnocarpa*

Dutch wings   Gasteria
Dwarf rubber-plant   Crassula argentea
Dwarf yew-plant   Podocarpus
Earth-star   Cryptanthus
Easter cactus   Schlumbergera Gaertnerii
East Indian holly-fern   Polystichum aristatum
East Indian ti   Cordyline terminalis
East Indian wine-palm   Phoenix sylvestris
Elephant's-ear   Caladium, Philodendron
   pertusum
Elephant's-ear fern   Platycerium angolense
Elephant's-ear plant   Alocasia, Colocasia
Elephant's-foot tree   Beaucarnea recurvata
Elkhorn   Euphorbia lactea cristata
Elk's-horn   Platycerium diversifolium
Emerald-feather   Asparagus Sprengeri
Emerald-fern   Asparagus Sprengeri
Emerald-ripple peperomia   Peperomia caperata
Erect sword-fern   Nephrolepis cordifolia
European fan-palm   Chamaerops humilis
Exotic fig   Ficus exotica
False aralia   Dizygotheca elegantissima
False cactus   Euphorbia lactea
False cypress   Chamaecyparis
Fancy-leaved caladium   Caladium hortulanum
Fan-maidenhair   Adiantum tenerum Wrightii
Fat-pork   Clusia
Feather-fern   Nephrolepis exaltata
   Whitmanii
Fern-asparagus   Asparagus plumosus, A.
   Sprengeri
Fern-balls   Davallia bullata
Fern-leaf aralia   Polyscias filicifolia
Fern-leaf inch-plant   Tradescantia multiflora
Fern-pine   Podocarpus
Fiddle-leaf fig   Ficus lyrata (F. pandurata)
Fiddle-leaf philodendron   Philodendron
   panduriforme
Fiddle-leaf plant   Ficus lyrata (F. pandurata)
Finger-aralia   Dizygotheca elegantissima
Finger-leaf philodendron   Philodendron
   Selloum
Fishtail-palm   Caryota urens
Five-fingers   Syngonium auritum
Five-leaf angelica   Aralia
Flame-nettle   Coleus
Flame-violet   Episcia reptans

Flamingo-flower   Anthurium Scherzerianum
Flat-palm   Howea (Kentia) Forsteriana
Flowering-fern   Osmunda regalis
Flowering inch-plant   Tradescantia
   blossfeldiana
Flowering-maple   Abutilon
'Fluffy Ruffles'   Nephrolepis exaltata
   Whitmanii
Foolproof-plant   Billbergia pyramidalis
Fruit-salad plant   Monstera deliciosa
Funeral-palm   Cycas
Geranium   Pelargonium
Giant-maidenhair   Adiantum trapeziforme
Giant white inch-plant   Tradescantia albiflora
   albo-vittata
Glory-fern   Adiantum farleyense
Glossy-leaf fig   Ficus retusa
Glossy-leaved paper-plant   Fatsia
Glossy-privet   Ligustrum lucidum
Gloxinia   Sinningia speciosa
Gold-dust dracaena   Dracaena Godseffiana
Gold-dust-plant   Aucuba japonica variegata
Golden-feather-palm   Chrysalidocarpus
   lutescens
Golden-old-man   Cephalocereus chrysacanthus
Golden-pothos   Scindapsus aureus
Golden-spines   Cephalocereus chrysacanthus
Golden-star-cactus   Mammillaria elongata
Golden-stripe sansevieria   Sansevieria
   trifasciata Laurentii
Golden wax-plant   Hoya carnosa variegata
Good-luck palm   Chamaedorea elegans
Good-luck-plant   Cordyline terminalis
   Sansevieria
Grape-ivy   Cissus rhombifolia
Graybeard   Tillandsia
Hair-palm   Chamaerops humilis
Hare's-foot fern   Polypodium aureum
Hatrack-cactus   Euphorbia lactea
Hawaiian good-luck-plant   Cordyline
   terminalis
Hawaiian ti-plant   Cordyline terminalis
Hawaiian tree-fern   Cibotium Menziesii, C.
   chamissoi
Heart-vine   Ceropegia Woodii
Hedge-fern   Polystichum aculeatum, P.
   setiferum

Saffron-spike   Aphelandra
Sago-fern   Cyathea medullaris
Sago-palm   Cycas revoluta
Saint-Bernard's-lily   Chlorophytum
Saint-John's-wort   Hypericum
Satin-wood   Murraya paniculata
Scarlet-basket-vine   Aeschynanthus pulcher
Scarlet-plume   Euphorbia fulgens
Screw-pine   Pandanus
Sea-teak   Podocarpus
Seersucker-plant   Geogenanthus undatus
Sentry-palm   Howea Forsteriana
Shrimp-plant   Beloperone
Sickle-plant   Crassula falcata
Silver-beads   Crassula deltoidea
Silver-dollar   Crassula arborescens
Silver-jade-plant   Crassula arborescens
Silver-lace-fern   Pteris argyraea
Silver-leaf-panamiga   Pilea pubescens 'Silver'
Silver-nerve   Fittonia argyroneura
Silver-net-plant   Fittonia argyroneura
Silver-star   Cryptanthus lacerdae
Silver-threads   Fittonia argyroneura
Slender-lady-palm   Rhapis humilis
Small-leaved-rubber   Ficus nitida
Snake-plant   Sansevieria trifasciata
Snowdrop-cactus   Rhipsalis Houlletiana
Snow-flower   Spathiphyllum floribundum
Solomon Island ivy   Scindapsus aureus
'Song of India'   Pleomele reflexa variegata
South American air-plant   Kalanchoë
    Fedtschenkoi
South American golden-barrel   Lobivia bruchii
Southern yew   Podocarpus macrophylla
Sow-bread   Cyclamen
Spanish dagger   Yucca gloriosa
Spanish moss   Tillandsia usneoides
Spathe-flower   Spathiphyllum
Spider-aloe   Aloe humilis
Spider-brake   Pteris serrulata
Spider-ivy   Chlorophytum elatum
Spider-plant   Chlorophytum elatum, Cleome
Spiderweb-houseleek   Sempervivum
    arachnoideum
Spiderwort   Tradescanthia
Spleenwort   Asplenium
Split-leaf   Monstera deliciosa, Philodendron
    pertusum

Spotted-dracaena   Dracaena Godseffiana
Spotted-dumb-cane   Dieffenbachia picta
Spotted-evergreen   Aglaonema costatum
Sprengeri   Asparagus Sprengeri
Sprouting-leaf   Kalanchoë pinnata
Spur-flower   Plectranthus
Spurge   Euphorbia
Squirrel's-foot-fern   Davallia bullata
Staghorn-fern   Platycerium bifurcatum, etc.
Star-cactus   Haworthia
Starfish-plant   Cryptanthus roseus
Star-leaf   Brassaia
Star-pine   Araucaria excelsa
Stink-bells   Fritillaria agrestis
Stone-crop   Sedum
Strap-fern   Polypodium phyllitidis
Strap-leaf   Caladium sagittifolium
String-of-hearts   Ceropegia Woodii
Striped-dracaena   Dracaena Warneckii
Striped inch-plant   Callisia elegans
Swedish ivy   Plectranthus
Sweet-basil   Ocimum Basilicum
Sweet-flag   Acorus Calamus
Sweet-marjoram   Majorana hortensis
Sweet-olive   Osmanthus fragrans
Sweet-orange   Citrus sinensis
Sweet-scented oleander   Nerium indicum
Swiss-cheese plant   Monstera deliciosa,
    Philodendron pertusum
Sword-brake   Pteris ensiformis
Sword-fern   Nephrolepis exaltata
Table-fern   Pteris
Tailflower   Anthurium
Tailor's-patch   Crassula lactea
Taro-vine   Scindapsus aureus
Tea-olive   Osmanthus fragrans
Tea-plant   Thea (Camellia) sinensis
Teaspoon   Crassula
Ten Commandments   Maranta leuconeura
Thanksgiving cactus   Zygocactus truncatus
Thatchleaf-palm   Howea (Kentia) Forsteriana
Thatch-screw-pine   Pandanus tectorius
Thousand-mothers   Tolmiea Menziesii
Ti-plant   Cordyline terminalis
Tiger-aloe   Aloe ausana, A. variegata
Toddy-palm   Caryota urens
'Tom Thumb' plant   Kalanchoë 'Tom
    Thumb'

Torch-plant   *Aloe arborescens*
Toy-cypress   *Crassula lycopodioides*
Treebine   *Cissus*
Tree-fern   *Cyathea, Cibotium, Alsophila*
Tree-ivy   *Fatshedera*
Tree-lover   *Philodendron*
Tree-of-kings   *Cordyline terminalis*
Tricolor-jade-plant   *Crassula argentea tricolor*
Tropic-laurel   *Ficus benjamina*
True-aloe   *Aloe vera*
Tufted fishtail-palm   *Caryota mitis*
Tuft-root   *Dieffenbachia*
Umbrella-palm   *Howea (Kentia)*
Umbrella-tree   *Brassaia (Schefflera)*
Uva-grass   *Gynerium sagittatum*
Variegated corn-plant   *Dracaena Massangeana*
Variegated-crassula   *Crassula argentea variegata*
Variegated-evergreen   *Aglaonema commutatum*
Variegated-grass   *Acorus gramineus variegatus*
Variegated-jade   *Crassula argentea variegata*
Variegated-philodendron   *Scindapsus aureus*
Variegated wax-leaf   *Ligustrum texanum variegatum*
Vase-plant   *Billbergia*
Veitch screw-pine   *Pandanus Veitchii*
Velvet elephant-ear   *Kalanchoë beharensis*
Velvet-plant   *Gynura aurantiaca*
Venezuela treebine   *Cissus rhombifolia*
Venus hair   *Adiantum Capillus-Veneris*
Victoria brake   *Pteris Victoriae*
Violet-slipper-gloxinia   *Sinningia regina*
Walking-anthericum   *Chlorophytum elatum*
Wall-fern   *Polypodium vulgare*
Wandering Jew   *Tradescantia, Zebrina*
Wart-plant   *Haworthia*

Warty-aloe   *Gasteria verrucosa*
Watermelon-pilea   *Pilea cadierei*
Wax-leaf   *Ligustrum lucidum*
Wax-plant   *Hoya carnosa*
Wax-plant, miniature   *Hoya bella*
Wax-vine   *Hoya*
Weeping-laurel   *Ficus benjamina*
Weeping-podocarpus   *Podocarpus elongata*
White-anthurium   *Spathiphyllum Clevelandii*
White bird-of-paradise   *Strelitzia Nicolai*
White-gossamer   *Tradescantia sillamontana*
White-plush-plant   *Echeveria leucotricha*
White-velvet   *Tradescanthia sillamontana*
White-wax-tree   *Ligustrum lucidum*
Wicker-ware cactus   *Rhipsalis (round stem)*
Widow's-tears   *Tradescantia virginia, Commelina*
Wild-olive   *Osmanthus*
Wild-pineapple   *Tillandsia fasciculata*
Wild-sensitive-plant   *Cassia nictitans*
Windmill-palm   *Chamaerops*
Windowed-plant   *Haworthia cymbiformis*
Window-leaf   *Monstera*
Window-plant   *Haworthia cymbiformis, Monstera deliciosa*
Wood-fern   *Dryopteris dentata*
Yellow-butterfly-palm   *Chrysalidocarpus lutescens*
Yellow-jasmine   *Jasminum Mesnyi*
Yellow-leaf dumb-cane   *Dieffenbachia 'Rudolph Roehrs'*
Yellow-old-man   *Cephalocereus Palmeri*
Yellow-palm   *Areca, Chrysalidocarpus*
Youth-on-age   *Tolmiea Menziesii*
Zebra-plant   *Aphelandra, Calathea zebrina, Cryptanthus zonatus*

*Abutilon* flowering-maple, parlor-maple
*Acorus* calamus-root
*Acorus Calamus* sweet-flag
*Acorus gramineus variegatus* variegated-grass
*Adiantum* maidenhair
*Adiantum bellum* Bermuda maidenhair
*Adiantum Capillus-Veneris* Venus hair
*Adiantum cuneatum* delta-maidenhair
*Adiantum farleyense* glory-fern
*Adiantum hispidulum* Australian maidenhair
*Adiantum pedatum* American maidenhair
*Adiantum tenerum Wrightii* fan-maidenhair
*Adiantum trapeziforme* giant-maidenhair
*Aechmea* (bromeliads) air-pine
*Aechmea fulgens* coral-berry
*Aeschynanthus* basket-plant, bog-rosemary
*Aeschynanthus pulcher* climbing-beauty,
    lipstick-plant, scarlet-basket-vine
*Agave americana* century-plant
*Aglaonema commutatum* variegated-evergreen
*Aglaonema costatum* spotted-evergreen
*Aglaonema Robelinii* painted-drop-tongue
*Alocasia* elephant's-ear plant
*Aloe arborescens* candelabra-aloe, candelabra-
    plant, octopus-plant, torch-plant
*Aloe ausana* tiger-aloe
*Aloe humilis* crocodile-jaws, hedgehog,
    spider-aloe
*Aloe striata* coral-aloe
*Aloe variegata* partridge-breast, pheasant-
    wings, tiger-aloe
*Aloe vera* medicine-aloe, medicine-plant,
    true-aloe
*Alsophila* tree-fern
*Anthurium* tailflower
*Anthurium Scherzerianum* flamingo-flower
*Aphelandra* saffron-spike, zebra-plant
*Aporocactus flagelliformis* rattail-cactus
*Aralia* five-leaf angelica
*Aralia spinosa* devil's-walking-stick
*Araucaria araucana* monkey-puzzle-tree
*Araucaria excelsa* Australian pine, Christmas-
    tree plant, house-pine, Norfolk Island
    pine, star-pine
*Ardisia crispa* coral-berry
*Areca* yellow-palm
*Asparagus plumosus* asparagus-fern, bride's-
    bouquet fern, fern-asparagus, lace-fern

*Asparagus Sprengeri* emerald-feather,
    emerald-fern, fern-asparagus, sprengeri
*Aspidistra* barroom-plant
*Aspidistra elatior* cast-iron plant, iron-plant
*Asplenium* spleenwort
*Asplenium bulbiferum* king-and-queen fern,
    mother-fern, mother-spleenwort,
    parsley-fern
*Asplenium Nidus* bird's-nest fern, nest-fern
*Aucuba* Himalaya laurel
*Aucuba japonica* Japanese laurel
*Aucuba japonica variegata* gold-dust-plant
*Beaucarnea* bottle-palm, pony-tail
*Beaucarnea recurvata* elephant's-foot tree
*Begonia* king-begonia
*Begonia Rex* painted-leaf begonia
*Beloperone* shrimp-plant
*Beloperone guttata* Mexican shrimp-plant
*Billbergia* natural-vase plants
*Billbergia leptopoda* permanent-wave plant
*Billbergia nutans* queen's-tears
*Billbergia pyramidalis* foolproof-plant
*Billbergia Saundersii* rainbow-plant
*Brassaia* Australian ivy-palm, Australian
    umbrella-tree, queen's-umbrella, rubber-
    tree, star-leaf
*Brassaia actinophylla* octopus-tree
*Brassaia* (*Schefflera*) umbrella-tree
*Caladium* angel-wings, elephant's-ear, mother-
    in-law plant
*Caladium bicolor* Corazon de Jesus
*Caladium hortalanum* fancy-leaved caladium
*Caladium Humboldtii* argyritis
*Caladium hybridum* imperial-caladium
*Caladium sagittifolium* strap-leaf
*Calamus* cane-palm
*Calathea insignis* rattlesnake-plant
*Calathea Makoyana* peacock-maranta,
    peacock-plant
*Calathea zebrina* zebra-plant
*Callisia* inch-plant
*Callisia elegans* striped inch-plant
*Caryota mitis* Burmese fishtail-palm, tufted
    fishtail-palm
*Caryota urens* fishtail-palm, toddy-palm
*Cassia nictitans* wild-sensitive-plant
*Centaurea candidissima* dusty-miller
*Centaurea gymnocarpa* dusty-miller

*Cephalocereus chrysacanthus*  golden-old-man, golden-spines
*Cephalocereus Palmeri*  yellow-old-man
*Cephalocereus polylophus*  bald-old-man
*Cereus peruvianus*  apple-cactus
*Cereus peruvianus monstrosus*  curiosity- plant
*Ceropegia Woodii*  heart-vine, rosary-vine, string-of-hearts
*Chamaecyparis*  false cypress
*Chamaedorea elegans*  good-luck palm, *Neanthe bella* palm, parlor-palm
*Chamaedorea erumpens*  bamboo-palm
*Chamaerops*  windmill-palm
*Chamaerops humilis*  European fan-palm, hair-palm
*Chlorophytum*  Saint-Bernard's-lily
*Chlorophytum elatum*  spider-ivy, spider-plant, walking-anthericum
*Chrysalidocarpus*  yellow-palm
*Chrysalidocarpus lutescens*  areca-palm, cane-palm, golden-feather-palm, yellow-butterfly-palm
*Cibotium*  regal-tree-fern, tree-fern
*Cibotium chamissoi*  blonde tree-fern, Hawaiian tree-fern
*Cibotium Menziesii*  Hawaiian tree-fern, man-fern
*Cibotium Schiedei*  Mexican tree-fern
*Cissus*  treebine
*Cissus antarctica*  kangaroo-ivy
*Cissus antarctica minima*  miniature kangaroo-vine
*Cissus Bainesii*  African tree-grape
*Cissus discolor*  begonia-cissus, begonia tree-vine, climbing-begonia, rex-begonia-vine
*Cissus rhombifolia*  grape-ivy, Venezuela treebine
*Cissus striata*  miniature grape-ivy
*Citrus mitis*  calamondin
*Citrus sinensis*  sweet-orange
*Cleome*  spider-plant
*Clivia*  Kafir lily
*Clusia*  air-tree, fat-pork, monkey-apple-tree
*Clusia rosea*  autograph-tree
*Coccoloba floridana*  pigeon-plum
*Coccolobis*  platter-leaf

*Coleus*  flame-nettle, painted-leaves
*Colocasia*  elephant's-ear plant
*Commelina*  widow's-tears
*Cordyline*  "dracaena"
*Cordyline australis*  palm-lily
*Cordyline terminalis*  East Indian ti, good-luck-plant, Hawaiian good-luck-plant-Hawaiian ti-plant, Polynesian ti-plant, red-dracaena, ti-plant, tree-of-kings
*Crassula*  teaspoon
*Crassula arborescens*  Chinese jade, silver-jade-plant
*Crassula argentea*  baby-jade, cauliflower-ears, dollar-plant, dwarf rubber-plant, jade-plant, Japanese rubber-plant
*Crassula argentea tricolor*  tricolor-jade-plant
*Crassula argentea variegata*  variegated-crassula, variegated-jade
*Crassula cultrata*  airplane-plant
*Crassula deltoides*  silver-beads
*Crassula falcata*  sickle-plant
*Crassula lactea*  tailor's-patch
*Crassula lycopodioides*  toy-cypress
*Crassula pagoda*  necklace-plant, oriental-tower
*Crassula rupestris*  bead-vine, buttons-on-a-string, rosary-plant
*Cryptanthus*  earth-star
*Cryptanthus bromeloides tricolor*  rainbow-star
*Cryptanthus lacerdae*  silver-star
*Cryptanthus roseus*  starfish-plant
*Cryptanthus terminalis*  pineapple-plant
*Cryptanthus zonatus*  zebra-plant
*Cyathea*  tree-fern
*Cyathea medullaris*  sago-fern
*Cycas*  bread-palm, funeral-palm
*Cycas media*  Australian nut-palm, nut-palm
*Cycas revoluta*  sago-palm
*Cyclamen*  alpine-violet, Persian violet, sow-bread
*Davallia*  carrot-fern
*Davallia bullata*  ball-fern, fern-balls, squirrel's-foot-fern
*Davallia canariensis*  deer's-foot-fern
*Davallia fejeensis*  rabbit's-foot fern
*Dieffenbachia*  dumb-cane, dumb-plant, mother-in-law plant, tuft-root
*Dieffenbachia picta*  spotted-dumb-cane

*Dieffenbachia* 'Rudolph Roehrs'   yellow-leaf
   dumb-cane
*Dizygotheca elegantissima*   false aralia,
   finger-aralia
*Dracaena*   cat's-claw
*Dracaena Draco*   dragon-tree
*Dracaena Godseffiana*   gold-dust dracaena,
   spotted-dracaena
*Dracaena indivisa*   dracaena-palm
*Dracaena Massangeana*   corn-plant,
   cornstalk-plant, variegated corn-plant
*Dracaena Sanderiana*   Belgian evergreen
*Dracaena Warneckii*   striped-dracaena
*Dryopteris dentata*   wood-fern
*Echeveria*   alabaster-plant, hen-and-chickens
*Echeveria elegans*   Mexican snowball
*Echeveria leucotricha*   chenille-plant,
   white-plush-plant
*Echeveria pulvinata*   chenille-plant
*Echeveria setosa*   Mexican firecracker
*Encephalartos Altensteinii*   prickly-cycad
*Episcia*   carpet-plant, lovejoy
*Episcia dianthiflora*   lace-flower-vine
*Episcia reptans*   flame-violet
*Eucalyptus*   Australian gum
*Euphorbia*   spurge
*Euphorbia Caput-Medusa*   Medusa's-head
*Euphorbia fulgens*   scarlet-plume
*Euphorbia heterophylla*   Mexican fire-plant,
   mole-plant
*Euphorbia lactea*   candelabra-cactus,
   dragon-bones, false cactus, hatrack-cactus,
   milk-stripe-euphorbia
*Euphorbia lactea cristata*   elkhorn
*Euphorbia mammillaris*   corkscrew
*Euphorbia (Poinsettia) pulcherrima*
   Christmas star, lobster-plant, poinsettia
*Euphorbia splendens*   Christ plant, Christ
   thorn, crown-of-thorns
*Euphorbia submammillaris*   corncob-cactus
*Euphorbia Tirucalli*   pencil-tree
*Fatshedera*   aralia-ivy, ivy-tree, tree-ivy
*Fatsia*   glossy-leaved paper-plant
*Fatsia (Aralia) Sieboldii*   paper-plant
*Fatsia japonica*   Japanese fatsia
*Ficus benjamina*   Java fig, laurel, tropic-laurel,
   weeping-laurel

*Ficus elastica*   India rubber-tree, rubber-plant
*Ficus elastica decora*   broad-leaved India
   rubber
*Ficus exotica*   exotic fig
*Ficus lyrata*   fiddle-leaf fig, fiddle-leaf plant
*Ficus nitida*   Indian laurel, small-leaved-rubber
*Ficus pandurata*   fiddle-leaf fig, fiddle-leaf
   plant
*Ficus retusa*   glossy-leaf fig, Indian laurel
*Fittonia argyroneura*   mosaic-plant,
   silver-nerve, silver-net-plant, silver-threads
*Fritillaria agrestis*   stink-bells
*Gasteria*   cow-tongue cactus, Dutch wings,
   lawyer's tongue, mother-in-law tongue,
   oxtongue
*Gasteria caespitosa*   pencil-leaf gasteria
*Gasteria hybrida*   bowtie-plant
*Gasteria verrucosa*   warty-aloe
*Geogenanthus undatus*   seersucker-plant
*Geranium*   crane's-bill
*Graptophyllum hortense*   caricature-plant
*Gynerium sagittatum*   uva-grass
*Gynura aurantiaca*   purple-velvet-plant,
   royal-velvet-plant, velvet-plant
*Haworthia*   cushion-aloe, star-cactus,
   wart-plant
*Haworthia Chalwinii*   aristocrat-plant,
   column-of-pearls
*Haworthia cymbiformis*   windowed-plant,
   window-plant
*Haworthia margaritifera*   pearl-haworthia
*Haworthia papillosa*   pearly-dots
*Hedera Helix hibernica*   Irish ivy
*Helxine*   angel's-tears, Pollyanna vine
*Helxine Soleirolii*   baby's-tears, Corsican
   carpet-plant, Corsican curse, Irish moss,
   Japanese moss, mind-your-own-business,
   peace-in-the-home, polly-prim
*Howea Forsteriana*   kentia-palm, sentry-palm
*Howea (Kentia)*   umbrella-palm
*Howea (Kentia) Forsteriana*   flat-palm,
   thatchleaf-palm
*Hoya*   porcelain-flower, wax-vine
*Hoya bella*   miniature wax-plant
*Hoya carnosa*   honey-plant, wax-plant
*Hoya carnosa variegata*   golden wax-plant
*Hypericum*   Saint-John's-wort

*Jasminum Mesnyi*   yellow-jasmine
*Kalanchoë*   Palm Beach bells
*Kalanchoë beharensis*   velvet elephant-ear
*Kalanchoë Fedtschenkoi*   aurora-borealis plant,
   South American air-plant
*Kalanchoë Fedtschenkoi marginata*
   rainbow-kalanchoë
*Kalanchoë pinnata*   air-plant, curtain-plant,
   life-plant, Mexican love-plant, miracle-leaf,
   mother-in-law, sprouting-leaf
*Kalanchoë 'Tom Thumb'*   'Tom Thumb'
   plant
*Kalanchoë tomentosa*   panda-bear plant,
   plush-plant, pussy-ears
*Kalanchoë tubiflora*   chandelier-plant
*Kentia (Howea) Belmoreana*   curly-palm
*Ligustrum lucidum*   Chinese privet,
   glossy-privet, wax-leaf, white-wax-tree
*Ligustrum texanum*   Chinese privet
*Ligustrum texanum variegatum*   variegated
   wax-leaf
*Lobivia bruchii*   South American golden-barrel
*Majorana hortensis*   sweet-marjoram
*Mammillaria campotricha*   bird's-nest cactus
*Mammillaria elongata*   golden-star-cactus
*Maranta*   arrowroot
*Maranta arundinacea*   obedience-plant
*Maranta Kerchoveana*   prayer-plant,
   rabbit-foot, rabbit-tracks
*Maranta leuconeura*   Ten Commandments
*Monstera*   window-leaf
*Monstera deliciosa*   ceriman, cutleaf-
   philodendron, fruit-salad plant,
   hurricane-plant, Mexican breadfruit,
   split-leaf, Swiss-cheese plant, window-plant
*Murraya paniculata*   satin-wood
*Myrsine africana*   cape-myrtle
*Neoregelia farinosa*   crimson-cup
*Nephrolepis cordifolia*   erect sword-fern
*Nephrolepis Duffii*   Duff's sword-fern
*Nephrolepis exaltata*   sword-fern
*Nephrolepis exaltata bostoniensis*   Boston fern
*Nephrolepis exaltata Whitmanii*   feather-fern,
   'Fluffy Ruffles'
*Nephrolepis Smithii*   lace-fern
*Nephrolepis Whitmanii*   lace-fern
*Nerium indicum*   sweet-scented oleander

*Nicodemia*   indoor-oak
*Notocactus*   ball-cactus
*Ocimum Basilicum*   sweet-basil
*Opuntia* (with flat stem)   prickly-pear
*Opuntia Ficus-indica*   Indian fig
*Opuntia mamillata*   boxing-glove
*Opuntia microdasys*   bunny-ears, rabbit-ears
*Opuntia microdasys albata*   angel-wing cactus,
   Angora bunny-ears
*Opuntia rufida*   cinnamon-cactus, red
   bunny-ears
*Opuntia Schickendantzii*   lion's-tongue
*Opuntia vestita*   cotton-pole cactus
*Osmanthus*   wild-olive
*Osmanthus fragrans*   sweet-olive, tea-olive
*Osmunda regalis*   flowering-fern, royal-fern
*Pandanus*   screw-pine
*Pandanus tectorius*   thatch-screw-pine
*Pandanus Veitchii*   Veitch screw-pine
*Passiflora*   passionflower
*Passiflora coccinea*   red-passionflower
*Pelargonium*   geranium
*Peperomia*   radiator-plant
*Peperomia caperata*   emerald-ripple peperomia
*Peperomia crassifolia*   leather-peperomia
*Peperomia dolabriformis*   prayer-peperomia
*Peperomia obtusifolia*   baby rubber-plant,
   pepper-face
*Peperomia obtusifolia variegata*   American
   rubber-plant
*Peperomia polybotrya*   coinleaf-peperomia
*Pelargonium odoratissimum*   apple-geranium
*Pelargonium quercifolium*   almond-geranium
*Pelargonium scabrum*   apricot-geranium
*Philodendron*   tree-lover
*Philodendron oxycardium*   cordatum-
   philodendron, parlor-ivy,
   philodendron-vine
*Philodendron panduriforme*   fiddle-leaf
   philodendron, horsehead-philodendron,
   panda-plant
*Philodendron pertusum*   breadfruit-vine,
   cheese-plant, cut-leaf, elephant's-ear,
   Mexican breadfruit, split-leaf, Swiss-cheese
   plant
*Philodendron Selloum*   finger-leaf
   philodendron

*Phoenix dactylifera*   date-palm
*Phoenix Roebelenii*   miniature date-palm,
   pigmy date-palm
*Phoenix sylvestris*   East Indian wine-palm,
   India date-palm
*Pilea cadierei*   aluminum-plant,
   watermelon-pilea
*Pilea depressa*   miniature-peperomia
*Pilea involucrata*   Pan-American friendship,
   panamiga
*Pilea microphylla*   artillery-plant
*Pilea nummulariaefolia*   creeping-Charley
*Pilea pubescens 'Silver'*   silver-leaf-panamiga
*Pittosporum Tobira*   Australian laurel,
   house-blooming mock-orange, Japanese
   pine, mock-orange
*Platycerium*   antelope-ears
*Platycerium angolense*   elephant's-ear fern
*Platycerium bifurcatum*   staghorn-fern
*Platycerium diversifolium*   elk's-horn
*Plectranthus*   spur-flower, Swedish ivy
*Plectranthus oertendahlii*   Brazilian coleus,
   candle-plant
*Pleomele reflexa variegata*   'Song of India'
*Podocarpus*   African pine, dwarf yew-plant,
   fern-pine, sea-teak
*Podocarpus elongata*   weeping-podocarpus
*Podocarpus gracilior*   African fern-pine
*Podocarpus macrophylla*   Japanese yew,
   Southern yew
*Podocarpus Nagi*   broadleaf-podocarpus
*Polypodium aureum*   hare's-foot fern
*Polypodium Meyenianum*   bear's-paw fern
*Polypodium phyllitidis*   strap-fern
*Polypodium vulgare*   wall-fern
*Polyscias Balfouriana*   Balfour aralia
*Polyscias filicifolia*   fern-leaf aralia
*Polyscias paniculata*   jagged-leaf aralia
*Polystichum acrostichoides*   dagger-fern
*Polystichum aculeatum*   hedge-fern
*Polystichum aristatum*   East Indian holly-fern
*Polystichum setiferum*   hedge-fern
*Pteris*   dish-fern, table-fern
*Pteris argyraea*   silver-lace-fern
*Pteris cretica*   Cretan brake
*Pteris ensiformis*   sword-brake
*Pteris serrulata*   brake-fern, spider-brake

*Pteris tremula*   Australian brake,
   poor-man's-cibotium
*Pteris Victoriae*   Victoria brake
*Rhapis excelsa*   bamboo-palm, lady-palm,
   large-lady-palm, little-lady-palm
*Rhapis humilis*   miniature fan-palm,
   reed-rhapis, slender-lady-palm
*Rhipsalis*   popcorn-cactus, wicker-ware
   cactus
*Rhipsalis cassutha*   mistletoe-cactus
*Rhipsalis cereuscula*   coral-cactus
*Rhipsalis Houlletiana*   snowdrop-cactus
*Rhipsalis paradoxa*   chain-cactus, link-plant
*Rosmarinus officinalis*   rosemary
*Saintpaulia*   African violet
*Sansevieria*   bowstring-hemp, devil's-tongue,
   good-luck-plant, hemp-plant, lucky-plant,
   mother-in-law plant
*Sansevieria trifasciata*   mother-in-law tongue,
   snake-plant
*Sansevieria trifasciata Laurentii*   golden-stripe
   sansevieria
*Schefflera*   queen's-umbrella
*Schefflera actinophylla*   Queensland
   umbrella-tree
*Schismatoglottis*   drop-tongue
*Schismatoglottis picta*   painted-tongue
*Schlumbergera*   crab-cactus
*Schlumbergera Gaertnerii*   Easter cactus
*Scindapsus*   devil's-ivy, pothos-vine
*Scindapsus aureus*   golden-pothos,
   hunter's-robe, Solomon Island ivy,
   taro-vine, variegated-philodendron
*Sedum*   stone-crop
*Sedum morganianum*   burro-tail
*Sempervivum*   live-forever
*Sempervivum arachnoideum*
   spiderweb-houseleek
*Sempervivum tectorum*   houseleek
*Sinningia regina*   Cinderella slippers,
   violet-slipper-gloxinia
*Sinningia speciosa*   Brazilian gloxinia, gloxinia
*Solanum Pseudo-Capsicum*   Jerusalem cherry
*Spathiphyllum*   spathe-flower
*Spathiphyllum Clevelandii*   white-anthurium
*Spathiphyllum floribundum*   snow-flower
*Strelitzia Nicolai*   white bird-of-paradise

*Strelitzia Reginae*   bird-of-paradise flower,
    queen's bird-of-paradise
*Syngonium*   arrowhead-plant, arrowhead-vine
*Syngonium auritum*   five-fingers
*Syngonium* 'Emerald Gem'   arrowhead
*Syngonium podophyllum*   African evergreen
*Thea (Camellia) sinensis*   tea-plant
*Tillandsia*   graybeard
*Tillandsia fasciculata*   wild-pineapple
*Tillandsia punctulata*   Mexican black-torch
*Tillandsia recurvata*   ball-moss, bunch-moss
*Tillandsia usneoides*   Spanish moss
*Tolmiea Menziesii*   mother-of-thousands,
    pick-a-back plant, piggyback-plant,
    thousand-mothers; youth-on-age
*Tradescantia*   inch-plant, spiderwort,
    wandering Jew

*Tradescantia albiflora albo-vittata*   giant white
    inch-plant
*Tradescantia blossfeldiana*   flowering
    inch-plant
*Tradescantia multiflora*   fern-leaf inch-plant
*Tradescantia sillamontana*   white-gossamer,
    white-velvet
*Tradescantia virginia*   widow's-tears
*Veitchia Merrillii*   Christmas palm
*Yucca filamentosa*   Adam's needle
*Yucca gloriosa*   palm-lily, Spanish dagger
*Zygocactus*   claw-cactus, link-leaf
*Zygocactus truncatus*   crab-cactus,
    Thanksgiving cactus
*Zebrina*   inch-plant, wandering Jew

## GOOD BOOKS ON HOUSEPLANTS

*Avocado Pitgrower's Indoor How-To Book, The,* 1965, Hazel Perper, Walker & Co., New York

*Bonsai, Saikei and Bonkei,* 1969, Robert Lee Beihme, William Morrow and Co., Inc., New York

*Citrus Seed Grower's Indoor How-To Book, The,* 1971, Hazel Perper, Dodd, Mead and Co., New York

*Exotica 3,* 1970, Alfred Byrd Graf, Roehrs Co., East Rutherford, New Jersey

*Ferns and Palms For Interior Decoration,* 1972, Jack Kramer, Charles Scribner's Sons, New York

*Foliage Houseplants,* 1972, James Underwood Crockett, Time-Life Books, New York

*Gardening In Containers,* 1972, Sunset, Lane Books, Menlo Park, California

*Gardening Indoors Under Lights,* 1971, Frederick H. and Jacqueline L. Kranz, Viking Press, New York

*Hanging Gardens,* 1971, Jack Kramer, Charles Scribner's Sons, New York

*Herbs To Grow Indoors,* 1969, Adelma Grenier Simmons, Hawthorn Books, New York

*How To Grow Houseplants,* 1971, Sunset, Lane Books, Menlo Park, California

*Indoor Gardens,* 1967, Ware Budlong, Hawthorne Books, New York

*Joy of Geraniums, The,* 1972, Helen Van Pelt Wilson, William Morrow and Co., Inc., New York

*Landscape Gardening In Japan,* 1964, Josiah Conder, Dover Publications, Inc., New York

*Making Things Grow,* 1972, Thalassa Cruse, Alfred A. Knopf, New York

*Pets and Plants in Miniature Gardens,* 1973, Jack Kramer, Doubleday and Co., Inc., Garden City, New York

*Saikei: Living Landscapes in Miniature,* 1967, Toshie Kawamoto, Kodansha International, Ltd., Tokyo, Japan, and Palo Alto, California

*Western Garden Book,* 1967, Sunset, Lane Books, Menlo Park, California

*Woman's Day Book of House Plants, The* 1965, Jean Hersey, Simon and Schuster, New York

# Index